Dictionary of Selected Forms
in
Classical Japanese Literature

Dictionary of
Selected Forms
in Classical
Japanese Literature

Ivan Morris

Columbia University Press

New York and London 1966

Ivan Morris is Professor of Japanese
at Columbia University.

Copyright © 1965 Columbia University Press
Library of Congress Catalog Card Number: 66-13020
Printed in the United States of America

To the Memory

of

Sir George Sansom

Contents

Introduction

The purpose of this dictionary is to help students to read
and translate classical Japanese literature; it is not
intended to be a definitive or systematic treatment of
bungo or an original grammatical study.

I have listed most of the forms that I have found in
my reading, giving examples from identified texts: the
earliest comes from Kojiki (A.D. 712) and the latest from
Tsurezuregusa (c. 1330), but the majority are from Heian
literature, especially Makura no Sōshi (43% of the 1,330
examples) and Genji Monogatari (17%). Several examples
have been taken from Japanese grammars and works of
reference and could not be studied in their full context;
their translations are consequently tentative.

The reader should remember how little we still know
about the distinctions that undoubtedly existed between
pairs like -KI and -KERI, TAMAU and TAMAERI. Much textual
work remains to be done before we can reach any reliable
conclusions about these distinctions, and we shall probably
never understand all the nuances. Here I have advanced no
theories of my own. Readers who are interested in having a
more systematic and interpretative treatment should consult
Yamada Kōyū's Nihon Bumpō Ron or Sir George Sansom's An
Historical Grammar of Japanese; on a more elementary level

Nakada Orio's Kammei Koten no Bumpō is a serviceable introduction, and I have referred to it for many of my examples.

As a rule I have used Japanese nomenclature to identify conjugations and inflexions. Foreign scholars are still far from agreeing in their translations of these terms. Renyōkei, for example, is variously given as "conjunctive," "Line II," "connective," "adverbial," "infinitive," "substantival," and "verbal." No doubt each of these descriptions has some merit; but surely it is far simpler, at least where the classical language is concerned, to use the Japanese name. Similarly shimonidan would seem to be a more practical identification for verbs of the tabu type than "2nd Conjugation" (Sansom), "Class I" (Vaccari), "vowel verb" (Bloch), and "Second Regular Conjugation" (Chamberlain). For the functions of words and affixes, however, I have used English terms such as "desiderative" and "negative" (instead of gambō and uchikeshi), since here the aim is explanation and description rather than identification.

I realize that many grammarians will object to the use of the word "past" as one meaning of kaisō and kanryō suffixes like -KERI and -TSU; but verbs with these suffixes are usually translated into some form of past tense in English, and it would be pedantic, if not actually misleading, to ignore the fact in a dictionary of this type.

x

Paradigms of verb and adjective inflexions are given
in Appendix I; the conjugations of all inflected forms in
the list are shown in Appendix II; Appendix III classifies
the principal entries according to the standard Japanese
system; and honorific, polite, and number forms are given
separately in Appendix IV.

The dictionary includes both independent and auxiliary
items of the type indicated in Appendix III, as well as
contractions, agglutinative forms, combinations of particles, and special constructions; it does not give ordinary
nouns, verbs, or adjectives that can be found in Japanese
dictionaries, unless they help to explain a particular
entry or are liable to be confused with other forms.

Frequently I have divided my definitions of words like
TO and NI into several numbered sections. These divisions
and their order are not based on any systematic linguistic
theory, but are purely for convenience and often arbitrary.
The meanings listed in the different divisions (e.g. YO 1.,
YO 2.) frequently overlap; conversely a single division
(e.g. NI 1.) will sometimes contain meanings so different
from each other that some authorities might prefer to put
them in individual sections. I have used no definite
criterion in deciding whether or not to list forms separately, but on the whole the separate forms are those that
(a) can be confused with other forms, (b) may be hard to

identify, or (c) have occurred with particular frequency in the texts I have consulted. Sometimes examples under the main (shūshikei) form may include other inflexions; thus the example for HABERI 1. is a rentaikei inflexion, and examples for OWASU 1. include mizenkei and renyōkei, as well as shūshikei, inflexions.

An important aim of this dictionary is to differentiate between homonyms and other confusing forms. I have therefore frequently included entries like -RAYU 2. (mizenkei of ragyō or rahen verb plus the passive suffix -YU), which might be confused with -RAYU 1. (passive suffix), while omitting parallel forms like -kayu (mizenkei of kagyō verb plus passive suffix -YU) that are unlikely to cause confusion.

I realize that my system of explaining compound forms (like -SHIKANARI) by reference to their constituent elements (SHIKU 2. -ANARI), which may themselves be compounds (ANARI = A 4. -NARI 1.), can involve a good deal of page-turning. It does, however, point up the importance of analyzing each form; besides, the alternative system of giving full, independent explanations under each entry would involve constant repetitions and make this dictionary at least twice its present length.

My thanks are due to Professor Donald Keene and to Dr. Marleigh Ryan for their valuable suggestions and help; to Professor William Skillend for his advice (mainly on the Manyōshū citations); to Mrs. Karen Brazell, Dr. Ryan, and Miss Mary Hue for their proofreading; and to Mr. George Buffington for providing about one hundred examples, mainly from Heike Monogatari and Hōjōki.

Students may be interested to see how this list can be used to analyze a sample passage from classical literature. The following are the first two sentences of Genji Monogatari; capitalized words, inflexions, etc. appear in the list.

IZURE NO ON-toki NI KA nyōgo kōi amata SABURAITAMAIKERU naka NI ITO yamugotoNAKI kiwa NI WA ARANU GA sugureTE tokimekiTAMAU ARIKERI. Hajime YORI WARE WA TO omoiagari-TAMAERU ON-katagata mezamaSHIKI mono NI otoshimesonemi-TAMAU.

IZURE: interr. pron. : which?

NO: possessive case part.

ON-toki
  ON-: hon. pref.
  toki: (noun) time, period

NI KA (2nd meaning)
  NI 1.: case part. = in, at
  KA 4.: adv. part. indicating doubt, uncertainty

nyōgo kōi: (nouns) Imperial Concubines (the nyōgo being of
    higher rank than the kōi)

amata: (adv.) in large numbers

SABURAITAMAIKERU
  SABURAI: renyōkei of SABURAU = "to be in attendance"
    (see Appendix II)
  TAMAI: renyōkei of TAMAU 1b. : hon. aux. vb.
  -KERU: rentaikei of -KERI : past or affirmative vb. suff.

naka: (noun) "middle, midst"

(N.B. nyōgo...saburaitamaikeru is a subordinate clause
    modifying naka.)

xiii

NI: (1st meaning) case part. = in, on

ITO: adv. : very

yamugotoNAKI: rentaikei of yamugotoNASHI (lit. "cannot be
    stopped") : impressive, dignified

kiwa: (noun) "social level, status"

NI: (1st meaning) case part. = in, on

WA: (1st meaning) case part. marking the emphasis inherent
    in a word or phrase (here it emphasizes the negation
    contained in aranu)

ARANU
 ARA: mizenkei of ARI, rahen vb. : to be, exist
 -NU: (2nd meaning) rentaikei of -ZU, neg. vb. suff.
 (N.B. rentaikei is used rather than shushikei because the
    word precedes GA 3.)

GA: (3rd meaning) concessive conj. part. : but, though

sugureTE
 sugure: renyōkei of shimonidan vb. suguru ("to excel")
 -TE: (1st meaning) renyōkei of -TSU 1. used adverbially

tokimekiTAMAU
 tokimeki: renyōkei of kagyō vb. tokimeku ("to flourish,
    prosper")
 TAMAU: rentaikei of TAMAU 1b. : hon. aux. vb.

ARIKERI
 ARI: renyōkei of ARI, rahen vb. : to be, exist
 -KERI: shushikei of -KERI : past or affirmative vb. suff.
 (N.B. mono ("person, one") is to be understood between
    tokimekitamau and arikeri : ito yamugotonaki...tokime-
    kitamau is a subordinate clause modifying this mono.)

Hajime: (noun) "beginning" (renyōkei of shimonidan vb.
    hajimu = "to begin")

YORI: case part. having same meaning as KARA 1. : from,
    since

WARE: pers. pron., 1st pers. : I

WA: (1st meaning) distinguishing case part.

TO: (3rd meaning) conj. part. marking end of subordinate
    clause : that (N.B. ware wa is an elliptical sub-

ordinate clause meaning "I (indeed) shall be ahead of
the others.") The vb. modified by the to clause is
omitted and some word like kangaete ("thinking") must
be understood (see TO 3a.); the omoi in omoiagari
cannot be taken to govern the to clause.)

omoiagariTAMAERU
  omoiagari: renyōkei of ragyō vb. omoiagaru ("to be proud,
    haughty, conceited")
  TAMAERU: rentaikei of TAMAERI, the -ERI (progressive)
    form of TAMAU 1b. : hon. aux. vb.

ON-katagata
  ON-: hon. pref.
  katagata: duplicated (plural) form of kata (noun) = "per-
    son, lady"

(N.B. hajime yori...omoiagaritamaeru is a subordinate
  clause modifying on-katagata)

mezamaSHIKI: rentaikei of shikukatsuyō adj. mezamashi
  ("vexatious, provoking")

mono: (noun) "person"

NI: (9th meaning) as if, like (same as no yō ni = "in the
  manner of")

otoshimesonemiTAMAU
  otoshime: renyōkei of shimonidan vb. otoshimu ("to des-
    pise, look down on")
  sonemi: renyōkei of magyō vb. sonemu ("to be jealous")
  TAMAU: shūshikei of TAMAU 1b. : hon. aux. vb.

Literal translation (essential additions in square
 brackets):

At which honourable period [was it that] in the midst of
the Imperial Concubines (of different ranks) [who] were in
attendance in large numbers there was [one] who although
she was (certainly) not in a very impressive social
position flourished outstandingly. The honourable
ladies who from the beginning had continued to be
haughty [thinking] "I (indeed) [shall be ahead of the
others]" [regarded her with] scorn and jealousy as a
vexatious person.

<u>Freer translation</u>:

It happened during the reign of a certain Emperor that
among the many Imperial Concubines of different ranks who
served at Court there was one who, though she did not
enjoy a very impressive position in society, was held in
particular favour. The other ladies, who had all been
proudly looking forward to securing first place in the
Emperor's affections, regarded this vexatious rival with
scorn and jealousy.

Abbreviations

Sources:

Eiga	Eiga Monogatari
GM	Genji Monogatari
Gosen	Gosen Waka Shū
Goshui	Goshūi Waka Shū
Hei.	Heike Monogatari
Hoj.	Hōjō Ki
Hyaku	Hyakunin Isshu
iroha	iroha uta (mid-Heian?)
Ise	Ise Monogatari
Izumi	Izumi Shikibu Nikki
Kag.	Kagura
Kage.	Kagerō Nikki
Koj.	Kojiki
Kok.	Kokin Waka Shū
Mak.	Makura no Sōshi
Man.	Manyōshū
MSN	Murasaki Shikibu Nikki
Nihon	Nihon Shoki (Nihongi)
Ochik.	Ochikubo Monogatari
Sagoromo	Sagoromo Monogatari
Sara.	Sarashina Nikki
Shinkokin	Shin Kokin Waka Shū
Shoku	Shoku Nihongi
Shui	Shūi Waka Shū
Tai.	Taiheiki
Tak.	Taketori Monogatari
Tosa	Tosa Nikki
Tsure.	Tsurezuregusa
Tsutsu.	Tsutsumi Chūnagon Monogatari
Uji	Uji Shūi Monogatari
Uts.	Utsubo Monogatari
Yam.	Yamato Monogatari

Other Abbreviations:

abbr.	abbreviation
adj.	adjective, adjectival
adv.	adverb, adverbial
app.	appendix
aux.	auxiliary
comb.	combination
cond.	conditional
conj.	conjunctive, conjunctival
const.	construction

Other Abbreviations (continued):

contr.	contraction
demonst.	demonstrative
desid.	desiderative
emph.	emphatic
equiv.	equivalent
esp.	especially
exc.	except
exclam.	exclamatory
hon.	honorific
impera.	imperative
incl.	inclusive
indef.	indefinite
infl.	inflexion, inflected
interj.	interjection(al)
interr.	interrogative
lit.	literally
loc.	locative
neg.	negative
obj.	objective
part.	particle
pers.	person(al)
plur.	plural
poss.	possessive
pref.	prefix
pron.	pronoun, pronominal
rhet.	rhetorical
sing.	singular
subst.	substantive, substantival
suff.	suffix
uninfl.	uninflected
vb.	verb
voc.	vocative

*   mainly or exclusively pre-Heian

** often or usually not translated

Dictionary of Selected Forms
in
Classical Japanese Literature

A

1. pers. pron., 1st pers.*

   <u>a</u> ga se (Koj.) : my lover

2. demonst. pron. : <u>that (place)</u>, <u>yonder</u>

   Awaji no shima no <u>a</u> wa to mishi tsuki (GM) : the moon-
   light by which one can see yon Awaji island

3. <u>mizenkei</u> infl. (follows stem of <u>yodan</u>, <u>nahen</u>, and <u>rahen</u>
   vbs.)

   shizuka nara<u>zarishi</u> yo (Hoj.) : a stormy (<u>lit</u>. unquiet)
   night

4. abbr. of ARU 1., ARI 1.

   hashitanaka<u>meri</u> (GM) (= <u>hashitanaku aru meri</u>) : it must
   have been unseemly

ACHI

demonst. pron. : <u>that (place)</u>, <u>yonder</u>, <u>beyond</u>

   <u>achi</u> no yama (Kag.) : yonder mountain

AGA

same as WAGA

   <u>aga</u> kimi yurusasetamae (Mak.) : I pray that Your
   Excellency will excuse me

   <u>aga</u> kimi (Mak.) : my dear ladies

-AKU

subst. suff. : see -KU 2a.

AMERE   A 4.   -MERE

   zuryō mo sa koso wa <u>amere</u> (Mak.) : a provincial
   governor [should] indeed appear to be thus

3

AMERI   A 4.   -MERI

ameri ka shi (Mak.) : there actually seem to be [people
who...]

warau mo amerishi (Mak.) : it appears that they (also)
laughed

AMERU   A 4.   -MERU

tanomoshige naru hito ni zo ameru wo (GM) : he certainly looks like a reliable man, but...

AN

abbr. of ARU 1., ARI 1.

to omoitannari (MSN) (= omoitaru nari = omoite aru
nari) : I thought that...

ANA

interj. of joy or sorrow : oh! ah! alas!

ana osana ya (GM) : oh, how young she is!

ana kura (Mak.) : oh, how dark!

ANARE   A 4.   -NARE 1.

onna wa san ni shitagau mono ni koso anare (GM) : a
woman (is a creature who) must respect the three
[dependencies]

Gon no Chūjō ni koso anare (Mak.) : it certainly appeared to be the Provisional Middle Captain

ANARI   A 4.   -NARI 1.

saba yokanari (Mak.) (= yoku aru nari) : in that case
it is all right

4

ANARU   A 4. -NARU 1.

    hito toru koto wa anaru mono wo (Tsure.) : and I hear
    they actually catch human beings

ANATA

  same as ACHI

    kita no shōji no anata ni (GM) : beyond the northern
    sliding-door

    anata no yoru mo (Mak.) : on the night before (lit.
    beyond) that one also

    anata ni makarite (Mak.) : I am going over there and...

    anata no hito mo konata no hito mo (Mak.) : the members
    of both the opposing team and of his own team

ANNARU   AN -NARU 1.

    annaru yama (Tak.) : a mountain that is said to be
    [there]

ARA

  mizenkei of ARI 1.

    Ajari no gen no usuki ni arazu (GM) : the Holy Teach-
    er's powers were considerable (lit. not shallow)

    kokoro araba (Hyaku.) : if you are willing

ARE

  1. same as A 1.*

    are koso wa yo no nagahito (Koj.) : it is I indeed who
    am the longest-lived man in the world

  2. same as A 2.

    are wa ta ga ryō zo (Mak.) : for whose benefit is it?

5

ARE (continued)

3. pers. pron., 3rd pers.

   are okose (Mak.) : awaken her

4. pers. pron., 2nd pers.

   are wa imamairi ka (Mak.) : are you a newcomer?

   are wa ta zo (Mak.) : who are you?

5. izenkei and meireikei of ARI 1.

   sōzōshiku koso are (Mak.) : it is sad indeed

   tsune naranu yo ni shi areba (Tsure.) : since this is
   indeed an ever-changing world

ARI

1. renyōkei and shūshikei of ari

   (a) rahen vb. : to be, exist, be located, have

   masanaki kotodomo ari (GM) : there are improper things

   shibashi arite (Mak.) : he stayed for a while and...

   (b) aux. vb. used for adj. conjugation (see -KARI)

   wazurawasetamau toki mo ōkari (GM) : many were the
   times when he suffered grief

2. intensive vb. pref.**

   arihatenu inochi (GM) : a (truly) endless life

ARU

1. rentaikei of ARI 1.

   kanashikaru hito (Uji) : people who are unhappy

2. adj. : a certain, one, a, some

   aru onna (Kok.) : a certain woman

6

ASHIKO

same as ACHI

ashiko ni komorinamu (GM) : I shall seclude myself
(over) there

ashiko made mo yukitsukazaruramedo (Mak.) : even though
it may not have reached its destination

ASOBASU

1. hon. yodan vb. : to do, perform, play

mari asobasu (Uts.) : His Excellency plays a game of
kemari

2. hon. aux. vb. (follows renyōkei)

kō wa kakiasobasarekeru (Hei.) : he wrote (was pleased
to write) this

ASOKO

same as ASHIKO

asoko no mine koko no hora yori (Hei.) : from yonder
peaks, from hither caves

-AUTE

-ai (renyōkei of vb. ending in -au) -TE 1. (ombin form)

naka no himegimi yori mo ōki ni mietamaute (Mak.) : Her
Highness looked bigger than the Middle Princess

go-taimen bakari saburaute (Hei.) : she will just have
an audience with Your Excellency and...

AWARE

1. subst. with a wide range of meanings : pitiful, moving,
etc.

sora no keshiki mo aware sukanakaranu ni (GM) : the
sky too was full of pathos

7

AWARE (continued)

2. interj. of entreaty, pity, grief : ah! alas!

aware samo samuki toshi ka na (GM) : oh dear, what a
(really) cold year it is!

BA

1. conj. part. expressing condition

(a) indef. cond. : if (follows mizenkei)

ōji wo hashiraba (Tsure.) : if one runs along the
highway

ume ga ka wo sode ni utsushite todometeba (Kok.) : if
one could transfer the scent of the plum blossoms to
one's sleeves and keep it there

kimi yuku to kikaba (Mak.) : if I had heard that you
were going

(b) definite cond. : when, whenever, since, as (follows izenkei)

mikotonori nareba (Yam.) : since it is the Emperor's
decree

ito aware nareba (Yam.) : as it was most impressive

isogeba ni ya aramu (Mak.) : no doubt because she is in
a hurry

N.B. following izenkei of -KI 3. or -MASHI 1., -BA
can also mean if, as in

mitamaemashikaba (GM) : if I had seen her

2. part of WOBA

onore woba shirazaru nari (Tsure.) : he does not know
me

3. concessive conj. (follows izenkei)*

ideji to omoeba (Man.) : though I thought they would
not come out

8

BAKARI

adv. part. expressing extent or limitation : only, just so much, nothing but, as much as, alone, merely, about; to the extent that, to such a degree

kashigamashi to omou bakari ni (Mak.) : to the extent that we found them noisy

mono ni ataru bakari sawagu (Mak.) : they were so excited that they bumped into things

Dainagon bakari no hito (Mak.) : a man of the stature of (or no less impressive a man than) the Major Counsellor

Satsuki bakari ni (Mak.) : at some time about the Fifth Month

hachikyūnin bakari ite (Mak.) : there were some eight (or nine) people [in the room]

hito ni omowaremu bakari medetaki koto wa araji (Mak.) : there can be nothing as delightful as being loved by people

fune ni norite ariku hito bakari yuyushiki mono koso nakere (Mak.) : sailors are really the bravest people in the world

nakanu bakari no keshiki nite (Mak.) : he seemed to be on the verge of tears and...

-BAMU

yodan vb. suff. expressing appearance, seeming, tendency, etc. (follows subst., renyōkei, or adj. stem)

nayoraka ni okashibameru koto (GM) : a tender and interesting-seeming thing

naebamitaru (Mak.) : they looked (or were somewhat) faded

uchimagirebami (GM) : looking at [him] in a stealthy fashion

9

-BARA

  plur. suff.

    hōshibara no nisannin (GM) : a few priests

    yatsubara (Hei.) : fellows

-BAYA

  desid. suff. : would that...! (follows mizenkei)

    torikaebaya (MSN) : would that I could exchange them!

    arasebaya to koso oboyure (Mak.) : they only wished
    that they could be

    kore ga koto wo kikabaya to omou ni (Mak.) : though I
    wanted to hear [their verdict]

-BEKAMERE   -BEKU -A 4. -MERE

    kita no mi-kado yori koso wa watarasetamaubekamere
    (Eiga) : it appeared that His Majesty would (certainly)
    enter by the northern gate

-BEKAMERU   -BEKU -A 4. -MERU

    henji wo mitsureba inochi wo nobubekameru (Mak.) :
    when one sees the reply, it seems as if one's life is
    going to (or can) be prolonged [so great is one's joy]

-BEKARAZU   -BEKU -ARA -ZU 1.

  1. neg. probability

    shizuka narubekarazu (Hei.) : it will probably be un-
    quiet

  2. neg. impera. or neg. desid.

    kyōyō wo mo subekarazu (Hei.) : let no masses be said
    for me!

    katamu to utsubekarazu (Tsure.) : do not play with the
    intention of winning

-BEKARI -BEKU -ARI 1.

sugusubeku namu arubekarikeru (GM) : they should let it
pass

kakute mo shibashi arinubekarikeri to namu oboehaberu
(Mak.) : I feel that I can go on existing just as I am
a little longer

-BEKERE -BEKU -ARE 3.

suzuro narubekereba (Uts.) : since it must have been
innocent

asu on-monoimi naru ni komorubekereba (Mak.) : since
tomorrow is a day of Imperial Abstinence and I must
remain in [the Palace]

namida mo ochinubekereba (Mak.) : since I was on the
verge of crying

-BEKI

rentaikei of -BESHI

shikarubeki furumai (GM) : such behaviour [expected in
the future]

-BEKU

mizenkei and renyōkei of-BESHI

shirubeku mo haberazarikeri (Mak.) : I could not know
it

-BEKUBA -BEKU -BA 1a.

samo arubekuba (Hei.) : in that case

-BESHI

shūshikei of -beshi, an aux. kukatsuyō adj. meaning might,
may, can, could, would, ought, will likely, shall, should,
must, etc. (but **) (follows shūshikei, exc. after rahen

-BESHI (continued)

vbs. when it follows rentaikei : e.g. kubeshi, but arube-
shi)

    osoku makubeki te ni tsukubeshi (Tsure.) : you should
follow the technique of trying to delay losing

    soragoto nado mo idekubeshi (Mak.) : they must have
told all sorts of lies

-BI

mizenkei and renyōkei of -BU

    uta sae zo hinabitarikeru (Ise) : even his verse was
provincial

    ikaga kotonashibi ni iiidemu (Mak.) : how could I give
a commonplace answer?

-BU

kaminidan vb. suff. meaning to have the attitude or condition of, behave like (follows subst. or shūshikei)

    otonabu (GM) : to act in a grown-up way

    otonabumeredo (GM) : though she seemed to act in a
grown-up way

-BURU

rentaikei of -BU

    ko no otonaburu ni (GM) : when children act in a man-
ner too old for their years

-BYŌ

ombin form of -BEKU

    ogi wo isaserarubyō ya sōrōran (Hei.) : it would prob-
ably be best, Excellency, to order that the fan be
shot down

hototogisu mo kage ni kakurenubyō oboyu ka shi
(Mak.) : one might really imagine that a hototogisu
must be hiding behind it

CHŌ

ombin form of TO IU

saku hana ni utsuru chō na (GM) : a name that is ap-
plied to flowers in bloom

-DACHI

1. same as TACHI 1.

nannyo no kindachi (Hei.) : the noble children, both
boys and girls

2. renyōkei of -DATSU

sugyōzadachitaru hōshi (Mak.) : priests who looked
like travelling monks

DAMO

adv. : as much as, at least, only, merely, even**

yume ni damo au (Izumi) : to meet even in a dream

DANI

same as DAMO

furisomuru kesa dani (Shinkokin.) : even this morning
when it has started [to snow]

hitome wo dani omowazuba (Mak.) : if I were not afraid
of being seen

-DATSU

yodan vb. suff. expressing tendency, appearance, condition (follows subst. or adj. stem)

Chūjōdatsu hito (GM) : a man who looked like a Captain
of the Guards

13

-DE

neg. conj. suff. (follows _mizenkei_)

Nijō In ni mo ara_de_ (GM) : he was not in the Nijō Palace, and...

mi_de_ arinubeshi (Mak.) : one should not see such things

DE FU

see CHŌ (the _ombin_ form of DE FU)

na_defu_ koto (Mak.) : what sort of thing?

-DO   see -DO(MO)

-DO(MO)

concessive conj. part. : _though_, _but_ (follows _izenkei_)

me ni wa sayaka ni miene_domo_ (Kok.) : though it cannot be seen clearly

mate_do_ mate_do_ (Mak.) : though they waited and waited

to notamawasure_domo_ (Mak.) : although Her Majesty said that...

-DOMO

1. plur. suff.

hito_domo_ (Mak.) : people

ko_domo_ no motekitaru (Mak.) : children brought them

ajiki naki koto_domo_ wo (Mak.) : there is really nothing interesting about all that

senzai_domo_ (Mak.) : the garden and so forth

14

tateru kurumadomo   (Mak.) : the carriages that were
standing [there]

2. same as NADO 2.

warebomedomo (Mak.) : something like self-praise

(see also examples 3-4 under -DOMO 1.)

3. see -DO(MO)

E

1. case part. expressing motion towards : to

kumo no nake e tachinoboru (Tak.) : to ascend into the
clouds

2. izenkei and meireikei infls. (follows stem of yodan and
rahen vbs.)

yukite kike (Mak.) : go and hear

on-suzuri no sumi sure (Mak.) : rub some ink on the
inkstone

subeki koto areba (Hoj.) : when I have something to
do

kono miyako no hajime wo kikeba (Hoj.) : from what I
hear about the founding of this capital

3. mizenkei and renyōkei of U 2.

ōku no monodomo roku ni etarikeru (Uji) : he acquired
many things as a reward

omoiwakarenu koso yokere (GM) : they praised it

4. neg. potential pref. (precedes main vb.)

ekoji (Koj.) : cannot come

e mo manebazu (Eiga) : cannot (even) learn

e kō wa arazarikemu (Mak.) : she cannot have been
like this

5. see WE

15

-ERE

<u>izenkei</u> and <u>meireikei</u> of -ERI

> mi wo shiri yo wo shirereba (Hoj.) : since I know my-
> self and know the world

-ERI

<u>renyōkei</u> and <u>shūshikei</u> of -eri, a progressive form (cor-
responding to modern -te iru) : is (was) -ing (N.B. -ri
is added to <u>izenkei</u> of <u>yodan</u> and <u>mizenkei</u> of <u>sahen</u> vbs.
e.g. <u>yome-ri</u>, <u>se-ri</u>; but historically the form is a con-
traction of -I I. -ARI l., and it is therefore conjugated
like ARI; -ERI does not follow other types of vbs.)

> kao wa ito akaku surinashite tateri (GM) : she was
> standing there, crying and rubbing her face till it
> was red

> kozo yakete kotoshi tsukureri (Hoj.) : being burnt
> down last year and built up this year

-ERU

<u>rentaikei</u> of -ERI

> toritsukitamaeru te wo hikinokete (Hei.) : pulling
> loose the hands that were clinging

> tateru kurumadomo (Mak.) : the carriages that were
> standing [there]

E SHI MO   E 4.   SHI MO

> e shi mo sumajiki (GM) : will undoubtedly not be able
> to...

-FU

<u>yodan</u> vb. suff. expressing repetition or continuation
(follows <u>mizenkei</u> of <u>yodan</u> and <u>shimonidan</u> vbs.)

> hana chirafu Akitsu no nobe ni (Man.) : in the plain of
> Akitsu where the blossoms are forever being scattered

konata kanata no kindachi kazu wo tsukushite owashima-
safu (Uts.) : among those who attended were young
noblemen who had come in great numbers from all over

GA

1. poss. case part.

   kari ga ne no kikoyuru sora ni (Kok.) : in the sky
   where one hears the cry of the wild geese

   ta ga ni ka aramu (Mak.) : whose can it be?

2. nominative case part.

   wa ga futari neshi (Man.) : we two slept together

3. coordinating conj. part. with extended use as concessive conj. part. : and; but, though (also sometimes used
   in the sense of because) (follows rentaikei)

   kataki ga (Mak.) : although it is hard

   oki no kata e oyogikeru ga (Hei.) : [the horse] swam
   out to sea, but...

4. desid. part. expressing hope, desire, etc. (esp. in
   combinations GA MO, GA NA, etc.) (follows rentaikei)*

   tatsu no ma mo ima mo etashi ga (Man.) : I wish I had
   a fiery steed at this very moment

   asa na asa na agaru hibari ni nariteshi ga (Man.) : oh,
   that I might become a lark that flies up [in the sky]
   each morn!

5. part. creating a phrase having the properties of an independent subst. (equiv. of modern no koto, no mono) (follows subst. or equivalent)

   Kakinomoto no Hitomaro ga nari (Kok.) : it is Kakinomoto no Hitomaro's

-GACHI

suff. expressing likelihood, prevalence, or predominance :
apt, prone, subject, liable to (follows subst. or renyōkei)

17

-GACHI (continued)

kumorigachi ni haberumeri (GM) : it seems to be cloud-
ing over

ito shimotogachi ni sashiidetaru (Mak.) : small
branches were growing luxuriantly from every part [of
the tree]

higegachi ni yaseyase naru otoko (Mak.) : a lean,
hirsute man

-GAMASHI

aux. shikukatsuyō adj., expressing appearance, impression,
or manner (follows subst. or renyōkei)

kayō ni hedategamashiki koto (GM) : the fact that we
seem to be separated like this

kagotogamashiki mushi no koe (GM) : the querulous
buzzing of an insect

ito waza to gamashikameri (GM) : it certainly seemed
to be on purpose

GA NA   see MO GA NA

GA NI   GA 1. NI 1. : in such a way that, in order to

oi mo tsugu ga ni (old folksong) : so that it may go
on growing

GARA

1. mizenkei of -GARU (follows subst. or adj. stem)

zaegarazu (GM) : not being inclined to learning

2. suff. expressing pattern, condition, design, character,
situation (follows subst. or renyōkei)

dai dashigara (Mak.) :[depending on] how you present
the subject

GARI

1. **renyōkei** of -GARU (follows subst. or adj. stem)

    otoko dani zaegarinuru hito wa ika ni zo ya (MSN) :
    what indeed can one think of a man who gives himself
    out as being very learned?

    sukoshi nasakegarikeru (GM) : he was inclined to be
    sympathetic

    netagariitamaeru sama (Mak.) : the way in which she
    looked cross

2. case part. expressing motion or location : to, at;
place, side, direction

    tsuma gari yukeba (Man.) : when he goes to where his
    wife is

    sa shitaru koto nakute hito no gari yuku wa yokanaru
    koto nari (Tsure.) : it is not good to go to people's
    places without any particular reason

-GARU

shūshikei and rentaikei of -garu, a yodan vb. suff. expressing sentiment, desire, inclination, affection, appearance : feel, fancy, desire, want; seem, pose as (follows subst. or adj. stem)

    wazurawashigaru mo omoshirokute (Sagoromo) : his feel-
    ing that he was being put upon was also amusing, and...

    sakashigaru hito mo aredo (GM) : though some people act
    in a knowing way

    nemugorogaru (Mak.) : she affects great amiability

-GATASHI

aux. kukatsuyō adj. expressing difficulty : hard, diffi-
cult to (follows renyōkei)

    tokegataku (GM) : being hard to understand

    kono yo ni wa haraigatage naru (Mak.) : it looks as if
    it could not be wiped clean in a whole lifetime

-GATE NI

suff. with same meaning as -GATASHI (follows <u>renyōkei</u>)

kaeri<u>gate ni</u> shite (Uts.) : finding it hard to leave

Inaminue mo yukisugi<u>gate ni</u> omoereba (Man.) : as I was thinking how hard it was to pass on through Inaminue

-GATERA

suff. expressing simultaneous action : to do a thing profiting from certain circumstances <u>or</u> while doing something else <u>or</u> on the way (follows sub<u>st</u>. or <u>renyōkei</u>)

imashime<u>gatera</u> ni iu koto : something said in the process of <u>admon</u>ishing (<u>or</u> incidentally to admonishing)

aki no no mo mitamai<u>gatera</u> (GM) : taking advantage [of the visit] to view the autumn fields

-GE

suff. expressing appearance, feeling, state, condition** (follows <u>renyōkei</u>, adj. stem, uninfl. adj., or subst.)

ayashi<u>ge</u> naru yuzu (Kage.) : plain-looking citrons

wakaki hito no okashi<u>ge</u> naru (Mak.) : an attractive young person

haruka<u>ge</u> ni iitsuredo (Mak.) : though they had given us to understand that [the procession] was far away...

GO-

hon. pref.

otodo no <u>go</u>za <u>go</u>mae ni ari (GM) : the Minister's mat was spread in front of the Emperor

GOHEN

pers. pron., 2nd pers. : <u>you</u>

<u>go</u>hen no chichi ko-Dainagon-dono (Hei.) : your father, His Excellency the late Counsellor

20

-GOTO (NI)

adj. or conj. : <u>each</u>, <u>every</u>; <u>whenever</u>, <u>at every time that</u>
(follows subst., <u>rentaikei</u>, or uninfl. suff.)

    kuru aki<u>goto ni</u> (Kok.) : each autumn (that comes)

    mae<u>goto ni</u> sue (Mak.) : placing one [tray] before each
    gen<u>tle</u>man

-GOTOKI

<u>rentaikei</u> of -GOTOSHI

    awa mugi mame sasage kaku no <u>gotoki</u> (Uts.) : things
    like millet, barley, soybeans, and cowpeas

-GOTOKU

<u>mizenkei</u> and <u>renyōkei</u> of -GOTOSHI

    kono uta mo kaku no <u>gotoku</u> narubeshi (Kok.) : this poem
    should also be like <u>that</u>

    saku hana no niou ga <u>gotoku</u> (Man.) : like the scent of
    the blossoms in bloom

-GOTOSHI

<u>shūshikei</u> of -gotoshi, an aux. <u>kukatsuyō</u> adj. expressing
<u>likeness</u>, resemblance : <u>seem like</u>, <u>resemble</u>, <u>as</u> (follows
<u>no</u> or <u>ga</u>, or <u>rentaikei</u>)

    Fune no ato naki <u>gotoshi</u> (Man.) : like a boat without a
    wake

    utsutsu ka to omoeba mata yume no <u>gotoshi</u> (Hei.) : when
    he asked himself, "Is this reality?" it again seemed
    like a dream

GOZEN

pers. pron., 2nd pers. : <u>you</u> (used to superiors)

    chichi <u>gozen</u> (Hei.) : your father

HA   see WA 1.-2.

HABERA

mizenkei of HABERI

yurusarehaberaba akete mihaberamu (Mak.) : if I were
permitted, I should (presume to) open [the letter] and
examine it

yomo haberaji (Mak.) : that hardly seems likely, Your
Majesty

HABERI

renyōkei and shūshikei of haberi

1. polite rahen vb. : to be in attendance, serve, come,
be

kumorigachi ni haberumeri (GM) : it looks cloudy,
Madam

2. polite aux. rahen vb. (follows renyōkei)

kano shiroku sakeru wo namu yūgao to mōshihaberu (GM) :
those white blossoms are called moonflowers, Your
Excellency

ima namu kaerihaberu (Mak.) : we are now on our way
home

yuzurihaberitsuru nari (Mak.) : they yielded it [to us]

HABERU

rentaikei of HABERI

to namu oboehaberu (Mak.) : I think (indeed) that...

(see HABERI for further examples)

HATA

intensifying or concessive adv. : indeed, moreover; however; possibly, perhaps

tachiyasuraubeki ni <u>hata</u> haberaneba (GM) : since I
must not hesitate, however...

-HATSU

aux. <u>shimonidan</u> vb. expressing conclusion : <u>to end by,</u>
<u>finish, reach a limit</u> (follows <u>renyōkei</u>)

    goranjihat<u>e</u>mu to oboshimesu ni (GM) : His Excellency
decided <u>to</u> see things through, and...

    imada omae ni wa idehat<u>e</u>de (Mak.) : they had not yet
all come (<u>lit.</u> fini<u>shed</u> coming) into His Majesty's
presence

HAYA

exclam. part. : <u>ah</u>! <u>oh</u>!*

    azuma <u>haya</u> (Koj.) : ah, my wife!

    kimi woba fukaku omou <u>haya</u> waga (Mak.) : oh, how deeply
I love my lord!

HIKI-

intensifying vb. pref.**

    hanatachibana wo <u>hiki</u>yojite oramu to suredo (Man.) :
though intending <u>to grasp</u> the orange blossom (firmly)
and break it off

    hito no fumi wo <u>hiki</u>torite (Mak.) a person snatches
away a letter

HODO (NI)

conj. : <u>when</u>, <u>while</u>, <u>as</u> (follows <u>rentaikei</u>)

    miru <u>hodo ni</u> (Mak.) : when one [goes to] see it

    yo uchifukuru <u>hodo ni</u> (Mak.) : as the night advanced

    kakaru tokoro ni sumai sesasetamawamu <u>hodo</u> wa (Mak.) :
at a time when Her Majesty was residing <u>in</u> such a
place

I-

1. vb. pref.**

   omou dochi _imurete (Man.) : being with a group of close
   friends

2. <u>mizenkei</u> and <u>renyōkei</u> of IRU

   kokage ni oriite (Ise) : having dismounted in the
   shade of the trees

   kono _itaru otona (GM) : this grown-up person who is
   [here]

   izuchi _inikeru (Mak.) : where can they have gone?

-I

1. <u>renyōkei</u> infl. (follows stem of <u>yodan</u> vb.)

   hana wa chir_i (Shinkokin.) : the blossoms scattered
   and...

   kimi ga yuk_i (Man.) : my Lord's journey

2. <u>mizenkei</u> and <u>renyōkei</u> infls. (follows stem of <u>kamiichi-</u>
   <u>dan</u> or <u>kaminidan</u> vb.)

   kyō sug_iba kono tsuki wa hi mo nashi (GM) : once today
   has gone, this month will have no more days

3. <u>ombin</u> form of -KI 3.

   karai me wo misaburaitsuru (Mak.) : a terrible thing
   has happened to me

IDE (YA)

interj. : <u>come!</u> <u>come now!</u> <u>let us</u>, <u>well</u>, <u>well now</u>, <u>look!</u>
<u>good gracious!</u> <u>forsooth!</u> <u>please</u>

   <u>ide</u>...osana <u>ya</u> (GM) : well, well, how young she is!

   <u>ide</u> sara ni ieba yo no tsune nari (Mak.) : truly, it
   sounds commonplace when put into words

ware ni yoki ki kirite <u>ide</u> (Mak.) : do please cut a
nice branch for me

IKA DE

adv. phrase : <u>by all means</u>; (with neg.) <u>on no account</u>

<u>ika de</u>...hito ni kikaseji (Mak.) : we must on no
account let people know

<u>ika de</u> kikihaberamu (Mak.) : I must hear it at all
costs

IKA DE (KA)

interr. adv. : <u>how</u>? <u>why</u>?

<u>ika de</u> saru koto nakute wa owashimasamu (Tak.) how
<u>will</u> you exist without it?

<u>ika de ka</u> toramu (Mak.) : why would they take [them]

IKA(GA)

1. adv. : <u>how</u>? <u>how</u>! (usually precedes <u>rentaikei</u>)

tsui ni wa <u>ikaga</u> naru to shirubeku (Kok.) : in the end
having to know how it happened

<u>ikaga</u> nikuki (Mak.) : how unpleasant it is!

2. interr. pron. : <u>what</u>? <u>how</u>? (usually precedes <u>rentaikei</u>)

<u>ikaga</u> omoubeki (Sara.) : what will you think?

<u>ikaga</u> omawazaramu to oboyu (Mak.) : one wonders how
they could possibly not love them

IKA NARU

interr. pron. phrase (<u>rentaikei</u>) : <u>what</u>? <u>what kind of</u>?

<u>ika naru</u> hito ka mono omowazaramu (Man.) : what kind
of person would not think of this?

IKA NI

1. interj. : <u>well now</u>! <u>come on</u>! <u>listen</u>! <u>look here</u>!

   ika ni Yoichi ano ōgi no mannaka ute (Hei.) : come now, Yoichi, try hitting that fan right in the centre!

2. adv. : <u>how</u>? <u>in what manner</u>? <u>what</u>? <u>why</u>? <u>how</u>! <u>what</u>! (usually precedes <u>rentaikei</u>)

   ika ni mietsuru yume ni ka arikemu (Mak.) : what can he have dreamt?

   ika ni omoikaeshitaru naramu (Mak.) : I wonder why they changed their minds

   ika ni wabishikaramu to mietari (Mak.) : what a sad spectacle!

   ika ni kokorouku tsurakaramashi (Mak.) : how sad and bitter it would be!

IKURA (KA)

indef. pron., adv., or adj. : <u>some</u>, <u>something</u>, <u>somewhat</u>, <u>a certain amount</u>

   mugen jigoku no kurushimi wa <u>ikura</u> hodo <u>ka</u> nankan to toitamaikereba (Hei.) : when he asked whether the torments of Hell were not rather hard to bear

IMASHI

1. pers. pron., 2nd pers. : <u>you</u>, <u>thou</u>*

   imashi mo ware mo (Man.) : both thou and I

2. renyōkei of IMASU 1.

   Abe no Otodo wa hinezumi no kawagoromo moteimashite (Tak.) : [His Excellency] Abe no Otodo brought the fur robe of the fire-rat and...

IMASU

1. shūshikei and rentaikei of <u>imasu</u>, an hon. <u>yodan</u> vb. meaning <u>to be</u>, <u>go</u>, <u>come</u> (= I 1. -MASU 1.)

ōfune wo arumi ni idashiimasu kimi (Man.) : you who set out on your great ship across the waves

2. shimonidan vb. having the same meaning as IMASU 1.

Uji e imasuru koto nao taehatezu ya (GM) : was it likely that he would have given up his visits to Uji?

hitokuni ni kimi wo imasete (Man.) : with you in another province

IMASUKARI

renyōkei and shūshikei of imasukari, an hon. rahen vb. : to be

imasukaritsuru kokorozashidomo (Tak.) : their intention in having been there

IRU

1. rentaikei and shūshikei of kamiichidan vb. meaning to be, etc.

yama ni iru kumo (Shui) : the clouds that are on the mountain

2. aux. vb. expressing continuation (follows renyōkei)**

hito ni tamawariitari (Uts.) : he was bestowing it on those who...

kokage ni oriite (Ise) : having dismounted in the shade of the trees

ITO

adv. : very; completely, most

ito tōtōki koto (GM) : how very laudable!

ITSU

adv. : when

itsu kimasamu (Man.) : when will you come?

ITSU MO

incl. adv. phrase : <u>always</u>, <u>ever</u>; (with neg.) <u>never</u>

  <u>itsu mo</u> <u>itsu mo</u> (Mak.) : for ever and ever

ITSU SHIKA   ITSU SHI 4. -KA 4.

1. indef. adv. phrase : <u>at some time or other</u>

  <u>itsu shika</u> to kasumiwatareru (GM) : [the treetops] had
become covered with mist (at some time or other <u>or</u>
without anyone's having noticed)

2. emph. interr. adv. phrase

  <u>itsu shika</u> to omoitaru (Mak.) : one wonders when on
earth [the day will come]

  <u>itsu shika</u> to matsu ni (Mak.) : while we were waiting
impatiently

IWAKU

subst. form of <u>iu</u> (<u>yodan</u> vb. : <u>to say</u>) (see KU 2a.)

  mizukara kokoro ni toite <u>iwaku</u> (Hoj.) : I look into my
heart and ask myself (<u>lit.</u> what I ask myself is...)

IZA

same as IDE

  <u>iza</u>...kataraitamaeba (GM) : come now, since you spoke
to me...

  <u>iza</u> tamae ka shi (Mak.) : oh, do come along [with us]!

IZUCHI

interr. adv. : <u>whither</u>?

  <u>izuchi</u> mukite ka (Man.) : turning in what direction?

  <u>izuchi</u> naramu to oboyure (Mak.) : I wondered where he
could be going

IZUKATA

same as IZUCHI

izukata ni motomeyukamu (Ise) : in which direction
shall I go to seek...?

IZUKO

interr. adv. : where? whither? whence?

harugasumi tateru ya izuko (Kok.) : where does the
spring mist go when it leaves?

izuko yori zo (Mak.) : where does he come from?

IZUKU

same as IZUKO

kono kani ya izuku no kani (Koj.) : where does this
crab come from?

izuku ni tatamu (Mak.) : where will they stand?

IZURA

1. interr. adv. : where(abouts)?

izura to mimawashitamau ni (GM) : when he looked about,
wondering where she might be...

izura tote (Mak.) : saying, "Where [are they]?"

iebito no izura to ware wo towaba (Man.) : if the
people at home ask where you are

2. interj. : what? how now?

izura to notamau ni (GM) : saying, "How now?"

IZURE

interr. pron. : which?

izure masareri (Shui) : which [of the two] is better?

29

IZURE (continued)

    izure wo yoki ashiki to wa shiru ni ka aramu (Mak.) :
how am I to know which is good and which is bad?

IZURE KA

 indef. pron. phrase : something or other

    izure no on-toki ni ka (GM) : during some reign or
other

IZURE MO

 incl. pron. phrase : both, all

    izure mo izure mo hare narazu to iu koto nashi (Hei.) :
it was perfectly clear in all directions

-JI

 1. vb. suff. expressing neg. probability, negative intention, or plain negative (follows mizenkei)

    yorozu no toga araji to omowaba (Tsure.) : if you
think that you will (probably) never make a mistake in
anything

    tada kano yuigon wo tagaeji to bakari ni (GM) : in-
tending, whatever happened, to respect his last
wishes (lit. not to violate)

 2. renyōkei of -ZU 2. (follows subst. form)

    goranjite (Mak.) : His Majesty, seeing [the cat]...

 3. shūshikei of certain adjs.

    aenaku imiji (GM) : it was discouraging and terrible

-JŪ   -JI 3. KU 1. (ombin form)

    imijū sesasetamau (GM) : they ordered [the ceremony]
to be performed splendidly

KA

1. pers. pron., 3rd pers. : <u>he</u>

   <u>ka</u> no ko (Man.) : his child

2. demonst. pron. : <u>that</u>, <u>this</u>

   <u>ka</u> bakari naru uchi ni (Mak.) : in a house like this

3. adv. : <u>thus</u>

   <u>ka</u> yuki kaku yuki (Man.) : going this way and that

4. interr. adv. part. used for interrogation, rhetorical questions and statements of doubt or uncertainty (follows and/or precedes <u>rentaikei</u>, but sometimes follows <u>izenkei</u>)

   ashi areba izuku e <u>ka</u> noborazaramu (Tsure.) : since [cows] have legs, where can't they climb? (i.e. they can climb anywhere)

   oruru <u>ka</u> (Mak.) : are you going down?

5. interj. part. expressing feeling, compassion, etc. (follows subst. or <u>rentaikei</u>)*

   ureshiku mo aru <u>ka</u> (Man.) : ah, how happy one is!

6. ending of <u>izenkei</u> of KI 3. (see -SHIKA 1.)

7. <u>mizenkei</u> of <u>yodan</u> vbs. ending in -<u>ku</u>

   yukamu to omoedo (Man.) : though he intended to go

KAI-

intensifying vb. pref.**

   unreshiki koto woba <u>kaiari</u> (Tak.) : to have happy things happen to one

   <u>kaikukumite</u> (Mak.) : burying himself [under his bed-clothes]

KAKARU   KAKU   -ARU 1.

   <u>kakaredo</u> nanoka arite (Eiga) : after seven days, however...

KAKARU (continued)

    kakarubeki chigiri (GM) : an appropriate vow (lit. a vow that should be thus)

KAKI-

  same as KAI-

    yagate kakiotoshite (Mak.) : immediately letting it fall

-KAKU

  aux. shimonidan vb. meaning to begin**

    sarugau shikakuru ni (Mak.) : beginning to tell jokes

KAKU(TE)

  adv. : thus, in this way

    kaku yuku (Man.) : going thus

KA MO

  1. interj. or emph. comb. of adv. parts (KA 5. MO 3.) expressing pity, compassion, lament, etc. (often used at end of poems) (follows subst. or rentaikei)

    ...kaze no oto no kasokeki kono yūbe ka mo (Man.) : ah, this evening when one hears the faint sound of the wind...!

  2. interr., rhetorical, or dubitative adv. parts. (KA 4. MO 3.) expressing questioning, doubts, etc. (follows and/ or precedes rentaikei or subst.)

    waga omou kimi ga mi-fune ka mo kare (Man.) : can it be my lover's ship - - that one over there?

    naganagashi yo wo hitori ka mo nemu (Hyaku.) : do you mean that I shall have to spend this long night alone?

KA NA

same as KA MO 1. (usually follows and precedes <u>rentaikei</u>)

...sumeru tsuki <u>ka na</u>(Shinkokin.) : ah, the clear moon when...

medetaku mo kakaretaru <u>ka na</u> (Mak.) How beautifully written!

mimaku hoshiki kimi <u>ka na</u> (Kok.) : oh, how I want to see you!

-KANARI   -KU 1.   -ANARI

hito no kokorozashi hitoshik<u>anari</u> (Tak.) : people's hopes are said to be all al<u>ike</u>

tsumi fukak<u>anna</u>reba (Hei.) : since his guilt was great

KANATA

loc. adv. : <u>there</u>

<u>kanata ni wa</u> nyōgo no kimi (Uts.) : and in the distance the lady's master

KANO   KA 2.   -NO 1.

demonst. adj. : <u>that</u>, <u>those</u>

<u>kano</u> kata ni haya kogiyoseyo (Tosa) : hurry up and row <u>over</u> there

ima <u>kano</u> kimi tachitamainamu (Mak.) : His Excellency (<u>lit. that</u> lord) will presently be taking his leave

<u>kano</u> hi no sōzoku (Mak.) : the costumes [that they <u>would</u> wear] on that day

-KANU

neg. potential aux. <u>shimonidan</u> vb. : <u>hard to</u> (follows <u>renyōkei</u>)

waga koi wa nagusamek<u>anu</u>tsu (Man.) : my love cannot be appeased

KARA

1. case part. expressing point of departure : **from**, **since**

   tada ima <u>kara</u> (GM) : only since now

2. conj. part. meaning <u>since</u>; <u>because of</u> (follows <u>rentai-kei</u>)

   akenu <u>kara</u> (Tosa) : even before dawn

   fuku <u>kara</u> ni (Kok.) : since the wind started

3. -KU 1. -ARA (follows adj. stem)

   aka<u>kara</u>ba (Goshūi) : if it is light

4. see MONO KARA

-KARADE   -KU 1.   -ARA   -DE

   hito sukuna<u>karade</u> (Mak.) : there were not a few people and...

-KARAJI   -KU 1.   -ARA   -JI 1.

   tsuyo okashi<u>karaji</u> to omou (Mak.) : they do not find it at all beautiful

   ureshi<u>karaji</u> ya (Mak.) : is he not delighted?

-KARAMASHI   -KU 1.   -ARA   -MASHI 1.

   ika ni kokorouku tsura<u>karamashi</u> (Mak.) : how sad and painful it would be!

   ika ni miru kai na<u>karamashi</u> (Mak.) : how little point there would be in seeing...!

-KARAMU   -KU 1.   -ARA   -MU

   wabishi<u>karamu</u> (Mak.) : they must be sad

   imiji<u>karamu</u> ame (Mak.) : the rain which must be very heavy

-KARANU   -KU 1. -ARA -NU 2.

  katachi nado yokaranedo (GM) : she did not look
  attractive, but...

  imada tōkaranu fune (Hei.) : a boat that was still not
  far out

-KARAZARI   -KU 1. -ARA -ZARI

  ika de ka ureshikarazaramu (Mak.) : how can one fail
  to be happy?

-KARAZU   -KU 1. -ARA -ZU 1.

  shintai yasukarazu (Hoj.) : he is uncertain whether to
  go ahead or to withdraw

KARE

1. pers. pron., 3rd pers. : he, she, it

    kare mihaberamu (Mak.) : I shall see him

2. demonst. pron. : that

    waga omou kimi ga mi-fune ka mo kare (Man.) : can it be
    my lover's boat - - that one over there?

3. -KU -ARE 3. (follows adj. stem)

    Hotoke no kazu shi ōkareba (Uts.) : since the number of
    Buddhas is large

4. KA 7. -RE 1.

    nagekaretsuru kokoro (Mak.) : my heart which had been
    [so] troubled

-KAREDO(MO)   -KU 1. -ARE 3. -DO(MO)

  hito mo ōkaredo (Hoj.) : though there were many people

-KARI   -KU 1. -ARI 1b.

  wazurawasetamau toki mo ōkari (GM) : many were the
  times when he suffered grief

-KARI (continued)

aware naru koto ōkari (Tsure.) : there are many moving things

nagokaritsuru umi (Mak.) : the sea, which had been calm

-KARIKEMU   -KARI -KEMU 1.

kitanakarikemu (Mak.) : they must have been dirty

-KARIKERI   -KARI -KERI

okashikarikeri (Hei.) : they were amused

hagurome mo madashikarikeru wo (GM) : since she was still too young to blacken her teeth

-KARIKI   -KARI -KI 3.

imijū okashikariki (Mak.) : it was extremely charming

-KARISHI   -KARI -SHI 3.

nowaki arakarishi toshi (GM) : a year in which there were fierce storms

okashikarishi mono wo (Mak.) : how delightful they were!

-KARISHIKA   -KARI -SHIKA 1.

...koso...yokarishika (Mak.) : it was certainly a good thing

sutemahoshikarishikaba (Mak.) : since they would have liked to discard them

-KARITSU   -KARI -TSU 1.

arakaritsuru kaze (Mak.) : the wind that was blowing violently

sōzōshikaritsuru ni (GM) : since we were feeling gloomy

36

-KARU   -KU -ARU 1.

   nani ka wa kurushikaru beki (Tsure.) : what harm can
   it be?

-KARUMAJI   -KU -ARU 1. -MAJI

   nikukarumaji (Mak.) : it would probably not be dis-
   agreeable

KA SHI

final emph. comb. of parts. (follows shūshikei and meireikei)

   arigataki kokorozashi narikemu ka shi (Tsure.) : it
   must really have been a splendid ambition

   hito no kokoro sawaginubeshi ka shi (Mak.) : they must
   certainly have been excited

   uchi ni iriitaramu hito woba shirade mo owase ka shi
   (Mak.) : His Majesty should really not have concerned
   himself with people who would (probably) live at home
   in retirement

   Uemo nado wa ie ka shi (Mak.) : Uemo, for instance,
   should certainly have said [something]

   mazu yome ka shi (Mak.) : first read it

KASHIKO

loc. adv. : there

   kashiko wa yarido narishikaba (Hei.) : since there was
   a sliding door (over there)

KA WA   KA 4. WA 2.

interr. or rhetorical comb. of parts. (usually expecting
neg. reply) (comes usually at end of sentence)

   kawaru wa hito no kokoro nomi ka wa (Kok.) : is it
   only men's hearts that change?

KA WA (continued)

nani shi ni ka wa... (Mak.) : why should I [do such things]?

ika de ka wa mairasemashi (GM) : do you suppose I would (lit. how would I) have let her come?

KA YA   KA 4.   YA 1.

ika ni to ka ya (GM) : what did you [say]?

KE

1. same as -GE

kanashike imo zo (Nihon.) : my sad love!

2. mizenkei of -KI 3. (see also SE 3.) (N.B. this is conjectural; KE 2. may instead be an abbr. of KERA)

suzuro naru nadomo wo tsukekemu (Mak.) : they must have named them indiscriminately

3. mizenkei and izenkei of kukatsuyō adj. (follows adj. stem)*

koto no shigekemu (Kok.) : many things to say

-KEKI

rentaikei of adjs. ending in -ke

takeki mono mo (Hoj.) : brave ones too

-KEKU

1. subst. suff. (see -KU 2b.)

Miyoshino no Yama no arashi no samukeku ni (Man.) : in the cold of the storm on Mount Yoshino

yo no naka no ukeku tsurakeku (Man.) : the sorrow and bitterness of life

2. __renyōkei__ of adjs. whose stems end in -__ke__

nodo__keku__ shite osore nashi (Hoj.) : it is peaceful and holds no fears

-KEMAKU -KEMU 1. -KU 2a.

katari__kemaku__ wa (Man.) : the fact of having told

-KEME -KE 2. -ME

Otodo koso yuki__keme__ (Mak.) : it is indeed the Minister who must have gone

toshigoro higoro mo areba koso ari__keme__ (Hei.) : after all these years [when nothing has happened] for him now to

sa koso wa oboe__kemedo__ (Mak.) : though they must certainly have felt like that

-KEMU

1. -KE 2. -MU

furi__kemu__ (Man.) : it must have fallen

kuchioshiku omoi__kemu__...ika ni nikukari__kemu__ (Mak.) : they must have been disappointed...and how bitter they must have been!

2. -KE 3. -MU

izure taka__kemu__ (Ise) : I wonder which is higher

-KERA

__mizenkei__ of -KERI

aoyagi wa katsura ni subeku narini__kerazu__ ya (Man.) : should they not have used the willow branches as chaplets?

saki__nikerazu__ ya (Man.) : will they not have bloomed?

39

-KERAKU   -KERI   -KU 2a.

so ga iikeraku (Tosa) : what he said

-KERASHI   -KERI   -RASHI

ama no kawa henarinikerashi (Man.) : the Milky Way
seems to have stood in his way

koko mireba ubeshi kamiyo yu hajimekerashi mo (Man.) :
when one looks at this place, one sees that rightly was
it established in the age of the Gods

-KERAZU YA   -KERA   -ZU YA 1.

see -KERA for examples

-KERE

1. -KU 1. -ARE (follows adj. stem)

aware naru koso okashikere (Mak.) : I was indeed interested to see how moving it was

2. izenkei of -KERI (follows renyōkei)

tatsu no shiwaza ni koso arikere (Tak.) : it is indeed
the dragon's doing

3. izenkei and meireikei of -ERI form of yodan vbs. ending
in -ku

kai yosekite okere (Man.) : you should be bringing (or
you must bring) up the shells and leaving (leave) them

-KEREBA   -KERE 2.   -BA 1b.

netaku tsurakereba (GM) : since she felt annoyed and
bitter

-KEREDO(MO)   -KERE 1.   -DO(MO)

ito nikuku haradatashikeredo (Mak.) : though it was
very annoying and we were angry

sama ashikeredo (Mak.) : though it is unattractive to watch

-KERI

1. shūshikei of -keri, a past, durative, or affirmative rahen vb. suff. (follows renyōkei)

   idekinikeri (Kok.) : it has happened

   akinikeri wagimo (Nihon.) : the dawn has come, my love

2. renyōkei and shūshikei of -ERI form of yodan vbs. ending in -ku

   to Sei Shōnagon ga kakeru mo (Tsure.) : as Sei Shōnagon also wrote

-KERU

1. rentaikei of -KERI 1.

   ametsuchi no akehajimarikeru toki yori (Kok.) : since heaven and earth first came into being

   saburaitamaikeru naka ni (GM) : among those who were in service

2. rentaikei of -KERI 2.

   see -KERI 2. for examples

KI

1. rentaikei of adj. (follows adj. stem)

   yoki hito (GM) : good person

   tōki wa (Mak.) : those who were in the distance

2. renyōkei of rahen vb. ku (to come)

   chokushi kite (GM) : an Imperial Messenger approached, and...

   idekikeru koto (GM) : the fact that she appeared

KI (continued)

3. shūshikei of -ki, an irregular preterite or perfective verb suff. (follows renyōkei; but note that after KU 3. and SU 1. certain forms of -KI 3. may follow the mizenkei, e.g. koshi hito = the man who came, ware seshikado = though I did it; but ware shiki = I did it)

oni no yō naru mono idekite korosamu to shiki (Tak.) : a devil-like creature emerged and tried to kill me

ato ni mo iiki (Mak.) : they also said it later

imijū soshiriki (Mak.) : they criticized it severely

mukashi Karu Daijin to mōsu hito ariki (Hei.) : long ago there was someone called Karu Daijin

-KIKOESASU

shūshikei and rentaikei of -kikoesasu, a humble aux. shimonidan vb. (= renyōkei of KIKOYU 2. -SASU 1.) (follows renyōkei)

nani ka wa hedatekikoesasehaberamu (GM) : why should I presume to withdraw?

machikikoesasuru ni (Mak.) : while I was waiting

KIKOSHIMESU

hon. yodan vb. meaning to hear, eat, drink, perform, rule, etc.

toku kikoshimeshite (Mak.) : [I hope that] Their Ladyships will finish their meal quickly

ue mo kikoshimeshite (Mak.) : His Majesty also having heard about it

KIKOYU

1. humble shimonidan vb. meaning to say, tell, inform

to kikitamaeshi to kikoyu (GM) : he informed [his master] that he had heard that...

2. shūshikei of -kikoyu, a humble aux. shimonidan vb.
(follows renyōkei)

    miyashiro no kata wo ogamikikoyu (GM) : to worship
(respectfully) at the Shrine

    konnichi no yuki wo ika ni to omoikikoenagara (Mak.) :
although I was wondering how you ladies [were enjoying]
the snow today

    kaesugaesu yorokobikikoyuru (Mak.) : I cannot tell you
how delighted we are, Your Reverence

KIMI

1. pers. pron., 2nd pers. : you, thou

    kimi narade tare ni ka misemu (Kok.) : to whom shall I
show it if not to you?

    waga kimi koso (Mak.) : my dear Madam!

2. subst. : Lord, Emperor, Excellency

    kimi ga yo ni (Shui) : in His Majesty's reign

    kono kimi to kokoroete (Mak.) : having an understanding
with His (lit. this) Excellency

3. subst. : gentleman, master, lord, lady

    atarashū kayou muko no kimi (Mak.) : the gentleman who
had recently been adopted as a son-in-law

    aga kimi (Mak.) : my dear ladies

    ito utsukushiki kimi zo (Mak.) : isn't she beautiful?

KIMUJI   see KINJI

KINJI

pers. pron., 2nd pers. : you, thou

    kinjira wa onaji toshi naredo (GM) : though you two
are the same age

KINJI (continued)

subete kinji ito kuchioshi (Kage.) : everything about
you is most pitiful

KO

1. demonst. pron. : this

ko shi yoroshi (Koj.) : this indeed is good

ko wa nazo (Mak.) : why this? (or what is the reason
for this?)

2. mizenkei and meireikei of rahen vb. ku (to come)

kochi ko (Mak.) : come here

yobedo yorikozu (Mak.) : though we called, he did not
come

KŌ(TE)

ombin form of KAKU(TE)

e kō wa arazarikemu (Mak.) : she cannot have been like
this

kōte yamamu ya wa (Mak.) : can we really end things
like this?

KOCHI

loc. pron. : here

kochi ko (Mak.) : come here

KOKO

loc. pron. : here

ōtono wa koko to iedomo (Man.) : though they say that
the great halls were there

KONATA

1. same as KOCHI

   konata kanata tsukuriokeru (Man.) : which they are
   making here and there

   konatazama ni mukite (Mak.) : facing this direction

2. pers. pron., 3rd pers. : he, she

   mazu konata no kokoro mihatete (GM) : first thoroughly
   examining her feelings

KONO   KO 1.   -NO 1.

demonst. adj. : this, these

   kono na (Man.) : this name

KORE

demonst. pron. : this (refers to both things and people)

   kore ni tsukete mo (GM) : in this regard also

   kore yori zo kikoetamau naru (Mak.) : you would have
   answered of your own accord

   kore ni oshieraruru mo okashi (Mak.) : it was amusing
   to have been instructed by him

   nao kore hitori bakari wa (Mak.) : at least let me in,
   if no one else

KOSO

1. emph. adv. part., often expressing impera. force** or
   strong desire (precedes izenkei)

   nao ayamari mo koso are (Tsure.) : there are definitely
   still mistakes

   ...to oseraruru ni koso asamashū nan no iwasekeru koto
   ni ka to oboeshika (Mak.) : when Her Majesty said this,
   I was [absolutely] astounded and wondered who could
   have spread the news

45

KOSO (continued)

2. voc. part.

Shōnagon no Kimi koso ake ya shinurame (Tsutsu.) :
Mistress Shōnagon! Is it daylight yet?

waga kimi koso (Mak.) : my dear Madam!

-KOSU

aux. yodan vb. expressing wish or command (follows renyōkei)

ume no hana yama no arashi ni chirikosu na yume (Man.) :
may the plum blossoms never be scattered by the
mountain storm!

KOTO NO

same as MONO NO

tada naru tokoro nite wa me tomarumajiki koto no
(Mak.) : though I would not have noticed her in an
ordinary place

KU

1. mizenkei and renyōkei of adj. (follows adj. stem)

ibuseku anazurawashiku omoiyararete (Mak.) : scorning
it as being uninteresting (lit. thinking of it scornfully as irksome)

2. subst. suff. following

(a) stem of the rentaikei of (i) verbs, (ii) verbal
suffixes with an intercalated -a- (kienaku, kinuraku,
chiramaku)

miraku sukunaku kouraku no ōki (Man.) : it is seldom
seen but often loved (lit. there is little seeing but
much loving)

(exception : with the suffix -KI 3. the whole rentaikei
is used, as in kitamaishiku = the fact of having come)

(b) adj. stem with -ke (see -KEKU 1.)

46

3. shūshikei of kahen vb. ku** : to come, approach, etc.

ware mo kono to yori idete ku (GM) : I shall come out
of this door too

okurete ku to mietaru monodomo (Mak.) : people who
looked as if they had come [after me]

KUDASARU

1. mizenkei of yodan vb. kudasu ("to give down," bestow")
-RU 2. : to condescend, hand down, bestow

Umaro to iu on-tsurugi wo zo kudasarekeru (Hōgen Monogatari) : he bestowed [on him] the sword called Umaro

2. hon. aux. shimonidan vb. (follows renyōkei or -TE 1.)

kyōtōra wo tsuitō subeki yoshi ōsekudasaru (Hei.) : His
Majesty vouchsafed to state (or was pleased to say)
that he [Munemori] would vanquish the brigands

MADE

1. case part. expressing point of arrival : as far as,
even, till (to the point or degree)

mutsukeki made sawagitari (GM) : it was chaotically
disturbed (lit. to the point of being chaotic)

Tsu no Kuni made (GM) : as far as Tsu no Kuni

2. conj. part. : until, by the time that (follows rentaikei)

hatsuka no yo no tsuki izuru made (Tosa) : until the
moon comes out on the night of the twentieth

MAHOSHI

shūshikei of -mahoshi, aux. desid. adj. (shikukatsuyō) :
wish to, should like to (follows mizenkei)

hito ni mo misemahoshi (Mak.) : I should like to show
it to people

koso...ito shiramahoshikere (Mak.) : I should certainly
like to know

47

MAHOSHI (continued)

takaku uchiidasasemahoshiki ni (Mak.) : though I was hoping he would [read] more loudly

orimahoshū narinuramu (Mak.) : you must be wanting to go to your room

on-irae no aramahoshisa (Mak.) : the[way] in which I wanted Her Majesty to reply

MAIRASU

1. mizenkei of MAIRU -SU 2.

ko no mochii mairasetari (GM) : he made them serve some "children's" rice cakes

to kakite mairasetareba (Mak.) : I wrote...and ordered it to be given [to her]

2. humble aux. shimonidan vb. (follows renyōkei)

koishiku omoimairasetamau (Tsure.) : I presume to love her

medetaku narite zo mimairasuru (Mak.) : I looked up to the Empress with a sense of real admiration

oshihakarimairasuru hito (Mak.) : a person who could imagine [the magnificent scene]

MAIRU

humble yodan vb. meaning to come, go, be, do, use, give, send, bring, eat, drink, try, close, open, etc.

mi-kōshi mairine (GM) : close the lattice

on-shitomi mo mairanu (Mak.) : Her Majesty's shutters have not been raised (opened)

on-kudamono mairi nado shite (Mak.) : [workmen] eating fruit and such things

mi-kushige mairite (Mak.) : the Palace hairdresser arrived

on-chōzu _mairu_ (Mak.) : they brought washing-water

In no mi-sajiki ni _mairitamaite_ (Mak.) : [His Excellency] went to the gallery of the Empress Dowager

-MAJI

shūshikei of -maji, an aux. _shikukatsuyō_ adj. with the opposite meaning of -BESHI, i.e. expressing neg. probability, negative future, etc. (follows _shūshikei_, exc. after _rahen_ vbs. when it follows _rentaikei_, e.g. _sumaji_ but _arumaji_)

Kara no mono wa kusuri no hoka wa nakutomo koto kaku- _maji_ (Tsure.) : one can dispense with (lit. probably not lack) all Chinese things except medicine

hoka wa _irumaji_ (Mak.) : no one else may enter

-MAJIGE   -MAJI -GE

kaze no oto ko no ha no nokori _arumajige_ ni fukimidaru (Izumi) : the wind sounds as if it were blowing so strongly that there could be no leaves left on the trees

ekakumajige (Mak.) : it appears that you will (probably) not be able to write

-MAJIKARI   -MAJIKU -ARI 1.

kyō no genzan wa _arumajikaritsuru_ (Hei.) : there was not supposed to have been an audience today

-MAJIKERE   -MAJIKU -ARE 3.

...koso sara ni eomoisutsu_majikere_ (Mak.) : I could not possibly have banished it from my mind

-MAJIKEREBA   -MAJIKU -ARE 3. BA 1b.

ama ni naritemo den no uchi wa hanaru_majikereba_ (Ochik.) : though she had become a nun, she would probably not leave the palace, and so...

-MAJIKEREDO -MAJIKU -ARE 3. -DO

   sa shi mo isogumajikeredo (Mak.) : though there is
   (probably) no need to hurry so much

-MAJIKI

 rentaikei of -MAJI

   motsumajiki mono (Tsure.) : a thing one should not
   have

   nadote tatsumajiki zo (Mak.) : why shouldn't we stay?

-MAJIKU

 mizenkei and renyōkei of -MAJI

   koko ni mo hito wa mirumajiku ya wa (Mak.) : do you
   imagine that there is no one to see you here (also) ?

-MAJIKUBA -MAJIKU -BA la.

   kono hito emanukaretamaumajikuba onore wo koroshitamae
   (Uts.) : if he cannot be invited, kill me

-MAJŪ

 ombin form of -MAJIKU

   tadotadoshikarumajū miyu (GM) : it did not look as if
   it would be uncertain

   te mo e sashiizumajū (Mak.) : I could hardly (lit.
   probably could not) stretch out my hand

-MAKU -MU -KU 2a.

   ume no hana chiramaku oshimi (Man.) : regretting the
   fact that the plum blossoms are about to fall

   kakemaku mo kashikoki kami (Mak.) : the deity whose
   very name overwhelms me with awe (lit. even the fact
   of putting it in words is awesome)

MAMA NI

conj. phrase with the meaning of

1. as, when, according to, on (as in "on seeing him"),
because, while (follows rentaikei)

  yo no fukuru mama ni (Mak.) : as the night wore on

  fune wo kogu mama ni (Tosa) : as they rowed the boat

  tsurezure naru mama ni (Tsure.) : when I am bored

2. as things are, in the existing condition, without change

  ari no mama ni mōsu nari (Hei.) : I must tell it
  (just) as it happened

  kore ga mama ni tsukōmatsuraba (Mak.) : if you do it
  just like this

MARO

pers. pron., 1st pers. : I, we

  maro ga chie (Koj.) : our knowledge

  maro ga musume nite (MSN) : being my daughter

  maro mo utamu to omou (Mak.) : I also want to play

-MASA

mizenkei of MASU 2.

  kodono nado owashimasade (Mak.) : His Excellency, the
  late [Chancellor], no longer being there

  waga seko ga kaeri kimasamu toki (Man.) : the time
  when my lover will come back

  kimi shi kimasaba (Shui) : if only you came

-MASE

1. mizenkei of MASHI 1. (follows mizenkei)*

  waga seko to futari mimaseba (Man.) : if I could watch
  it together with my husband

51

-MASE (continued)

2. <u>izenkei</u> and <u>meireikei</u> of MASU 2. (follows <u>renyōkei</u>)

owashi<u>mase</u>ba (Mak.) : since His Majesty was there

shibashi goranjite owashi<u>mase</u> (Mak.) : would it please you to stay and watch for a while?

toburaiki<u>mase</u> (Kok.) : come and visit me

-MASEBA

1. -MASE 1. -BA 1a.

waga seko to futari mi<u>maseba</u> (Man.) : if I could watch it together with my husband

2. -MASE 2. -BA 1b.

owashi<u>maseba</u> (Mak.) : since His Majesty was present

MASHI

1. <u>shūshikei</u> and <u>rentaikei</u> of -mashi, aux. irregular adj. expressing doubt, vague probability, conjecture, presumption, hypothetical state; desire, intention, wish : <u>would (have), ought to have, might have, should like to, would that</u>! (often used in apodosis of cond. sentences) (follows <u>mizenkei</u>)

motometamawashikaba iraete<u>mashi</u> (Mak.) : if you had asked, they would have replied

saka<u>mashi</u> (Kok.) : would that they might scatter!

kesa no sama ika ni habera<u>mashi</u> (Mak.) : what would it look like this morning?

ika ni shira<u>mashi</u> (Mak.) : how could I know it?

kore ni nani wo kaka<u>mashi</u> (Mak.) : what shall we write in these [notebooks]?

2. pers. pron., 2nd pers. : <u>you</u>, <u>thou</u> (cf. IMASHI, MIMASHI)*

<u>mashi</u> mo ware mo (Man.) : both thou and I

3. renyōkei of MASU

owashimashinu (GM) : His Highness proceeded

-MASHIJI

same as -MAJI*

wasurayumashiji (Man.) : I cannot forget it

-MASHIKA

izenkei of MASHI 1.

uta koso yomamashika (Mak.) : I would certainly have
written a poem

mōsazaremashikaba (Mak.) : if I had not said it

-MASHI MONO WO   MASHI 1. MONO WO 2.

kimi ga yumi ni mo naramashi mono wo (Man.) : oh, that
I might become your bow!

-MASHI WO   MASHI 1. WO 3.

ami sasamashi wo (Man.) : oh, that I might net [a
bird]!

ki mo towamashi wo (Man.) : oh, that she might come and
ask!

MASU

1. yodan vb. : to dwell, be, go

kashiwagi ni hamori no kami wa masazu tomo (GM) : even
though the leaf guardian deity does not dwell in the
oak tree

2. hon. aux. yodan vb. (follows renyōkei)

Go no Miya itsutsu mutsu ni arishimaseba (Eiga) : since
the Fifth Princess was [only] about five years old

kaku waraimasu ga hazukashi (Mak.) : it is shameful
that you ladies should laugh like that

MATSURU

1. yodan vb. : to give (to a superior)

   kimi ni matsuraba (Man.) : if I give it to my
   lord

2. humble aux. vb. (follows renyōkei)

   tsukaematsuramu yorozu yo made ni (Man.) : we shall
   serve, yes, for ever and ever

-ME

izenkei of -MU

   utate koso arame (GM) : it is indeed terrible

   kokoro shirazaramu mono koso tsutsumame (Mak.) : a
   person who is unfamiliar with the way in which things
   are done might indeed be reserved

   ware koime ya mo (Shui) : [in that case] would I languish for you [as I do]?

-MEKASHI

shūshikei of -mekashi, adj. suff. (shikukatsuyō) expressing appearance, etc. : savouring of, characterized by,
-ish (follows subst., uninfl. adj., or rentaikei)

   mi no ue medetaku imamekashi (Uts.) : he was splendidly
   up-to-date

-MEKU

aux. yodan vb. expressing appearance, etc. (follows subst.
or adj. stem)

   tsumimekitaru on-yamai ni mo arazamerikereba (GM) :
   since it did not look like a guilty-seeming
   illness

   karamekite okashi (Mak.) : it was done attractively in
   the Chinese style

54

-MERE

izenkei of -MERI

hitogoto ni iumeredo (Tsure.) : though people always (seem to) say

warokamereba (Mak.) : because it is (or seems to be) bad

-MERI

shūshikei and renyōkei of -meri, aux. rahen vb. expressing futurity, seeming, slight uncertainty, probability, etc. (follows shūshikei, exc. after rahen vbs. when it follows rentaikei, e.g. kumeri but haberumeri)

motemairumeri (Mak.) : I believe that they brought it

mina nakumeri (Mak.) : everyone cried

hodo no sebakereba nameri (Mak.) (= narumeri) : this was probably because the place was so cramped

-MERU

rentaikei of -MERI

tenka narumeru (Hei.) : the whole world seemed to groan

MESU

shūshikei and rentaikei of -mesu

1. hon. yodan vb. : to see; call, summon, send for, procure; eat, drink; wear; ride; buy; do

meseba mikotae shite okitareba (GM) : when he sent for [a servant] the man answered and got up

2. hon. aux. yodan vb. (follows renyōkei)

omōshimesu na (Man.) : pray do not think

kikoshimesazarikeru (Eiga) : Her Majesty did not mention it

MI

1. hon. pref. : august, honourable**

   mi-ko sae umaretamainu (GM) : a young prince has been born

   mi-koshi (Mak.) : palanquin

   mi-kōshi (Mak.) : lattice

   mi-gushi (Mak.) : hair

2. following stem of adj.

   (a) subst. suff.

   sora samumi (Mak.) : the coldness of the sky

   shiranami (Shui) : ignorance (lit. the fact of not knowing)

   (b) suff. having the sense of conj. because

   se wo hayami (Hyaku) : because the rapids are [so] swift

   yama fukami (Shinkokin) : because the mountains are [so] deep

3. mizenkei and renyōkei of kamiichidan vb. miru ("to see")

   mitatematsuranu wa (GM) : if I do not see you

MIMASHI

pers. pron., 2nd pers. : thou, you (respectful)*

   mimashi Fujiwara Ason (Shoku) : thou, Lord Fujiwara

MO

1. inclusive, exclusive, or weak emphatic part. : also, too, even**

   uguisu wa fumi nado ni mo medetaki mono ni tsukurite (Mak.) : the nightingale is praised also (or even) in Chinese verse

ta mo...to nomi koso haberumere (Mak.) : indeed they
all seem only to think...

2. concessive conj. part. : though, notwithstanding (follows rentaikei or -TE 1. or -KU 1.)

ge ni irihatetemo (GM) : though you actually succeed in
entering

yamaji shirazu mo (Man.) : even though I do not know
the mountain paths

idetaru mo kai ya nakaramu (Kage.) : though they
blossomed out, it cannot have been of any use

Naniwa Watari no tōkaranu mo (Mak.) : though the Ford
of Naniwa may not be far away

3. interj. part. (follows shūshikei)*

uguisu naku mo (Man.) : ah, the nightingale sings!

MO GA   MO 3. GA 4. : desid. comb. of parts.

waga tsuma mo e ni kakitoramu izuma mo ga (Man.) : oh,
that I had the time to draw my wife!

MO GA MO

same as MO GA

misemu ko mo ga mo (Man.) : oh, for my darling [wife]
to show it to!

MO GA NA   MO 3. GA 4. NA 5. : desid. comb. of parts.

yo no naka ni saranu wakare no naku mo ga na (Kok.) :
oh, that our life might be free from the inevitable
parting (i.e. death)!

hito ni kataritsubekaramu nite mo ga na to omou
(Mak.) : they had hoped [to meet] people who would
tell about them

saramu hito mo ga na (Mak.) : if only there were such
people!

MO KOSO   MO 1.   KOSO : comb. of parts. with meanings of
I hope not (cf. modern suru to komaru), what
if...? it may well be...! etc. (cf. modern ka mo
shirenai)

hizō ni okashiki koto mo koso are (Mak.) : what if it
is something utterly strange?

karasu nado mo koso mitsukure (GM) : I only hope the
crows will not find it

ayamari mo koso are (Tsure.) : let us hope you make no
mistake

MO...MO

balancing adv. constr. : both...and, neither...nor

ashiku mo yoku mo (GM) : both badly and well

kuruma nite mo kachi nite mo (Mak.) : both in a
carriage and on foot

MONO KA

mono ("thing") KA 5. : interj. phrase

mau mono ka (Mak.) : she actually danced

MONO KARA

1. concessive constr. : although, while (follows rentaikei)

tsuki wa ariake nite hikari wo samareru mono kara
(GM) : though the dawn light weakened the moon's
rays

kaerigoto wa sakashira ni uchisuru mono kara (Mak.) :
although he produced a pretentious reply

2. and, moreover, in addition

etsugasetamawazaramu mono kara (GM) : you cannot
follow [in his footsteps], and moreover...

MONO NO

1. same as MONO KARA

   tanomanu mono no koitsutsu zo nuru (Ise) : though I
   have no expectations, I go to bed with loving thoughts

   mi-yuki wa medetaki mono no (Mak.) : though an Imperial
   Procession is a splendid thing

2. mono (subst. meaning "thing") NO 1.**

   e ni kakitaru mono no himegimi (MSN) : the [type of]
   princess one sees in pictures

MONO SU

sahen vb. with meanings of to be, go, come; write, say;
have; do, make; eat, etc.

   to mono seyo (Tsutsu.) : let us say that...

   soko ni mono suru hodo naraba (GM) : if it is while he
   is there

   roku no koto mono shihaberamu (Mak.) : I am going to
   give instructions about [the messenger's] reward

MONO WO

1. same as MONO KARA

   chiru to mite aru beki mono wo (Kok.) : when I saw that
   the blossoms had scattered, I should have accepted it
   with resignation, but...

   Dainagon ni mo masaritamaeru mono wo (Mak.) : though he
   excelled even the Major Counsellor

2. mono (subst. meaning "thing") WO 3. : interj. constr.

   sa bakari imashimetsuru mono wo (Mak.) : to think that
   I warned them so [carefully]!

   kimi to oramashi mono wo (Man.) : oh, that I might be
   with you!

   okashikarishi mono wo (Mak.) : oh, how delightful they
   were!

MONO YUE

same as MONO KARA

matsu hito mo konu mono yue ni (Kok.) : though the
person I was waiting for did not come

MOSHI

1. cond. conj. : if

kimi ga yuki moshi hisa naraba (Man.) : if you are gone
for a long time

2. adv.

(a) maybe, possibly, by any chance

moshi jōgan no uchi nite esasetamaeru ka (Mak.) : can
it (possibly) be that you have received it from some
member of the Great Council?

(b) else, otherwise

moshi wa...ashibukuro nado mo ie ka shi (Mak.) : or
else they should be called something like "leg
bags"

MŌSU

1. yodan vb. meaning to speak, say (humble)

mōshishirasureba (GM) : when he informed His
Excellency

2. humble aux. vb. (follows renyōkei)

iroiro no gan hatashimōsubeki yoshi (GM) : that he
would carry out all His Excellency's wishes

kore wo koso karimōsubekarikere (Mak.) : we should
certainly have borrowed this from you

...yorokobimōshihaberu (Mak.) : it delights me, Madam,
that...

MOTE-

intensifying vb. pref., sometimes indicating continuation
of act**

waga okotari nite wa motesokonawaji (GM) : she would
not cause him any harm by her own negligence

yuki moteyukeba (Mak.) : we went on and on

ya no motehanarete (Mak.) : the arrow goes astray
and...

MO YA   see WA MO YA

MO ZO

same as MO KOSO

ame mo zo furu (Tsure.) : I hope it will not rain

-MU

shūshikei and rentaikei of -mu, aux. yodan vb. with same
general meaning as -MASHI 1., expressing probability, intention, wish, anticipation, or prediction; conjecture
of past action; also hortative : probably, will; let us
(follows mizenkei)

tsuyu tagawazaramu to ukagaiitaramu wa (Tsure.) :
if in your dealings with people you expect never to
go against them

yagate mimu (Mak.) : let us [go and] see
directly!

imijikaramu ame (Mak.) : the rain which must be very
heavy

mieba warawamu (Mak.) : when I see him, I shall
laugh

imo wo motomemu (Man.) : I want to seek my love

sore kikamu (Mak.) : I should like to hear them

61

-MU NI   -MU NI 2. : conj. const.

1. <u>if</u>, <u>because</u>

yoku omoietaramu ni mo (Mak.) : even if I had been able to think <u>of</u> something suitable

sara ni owasemu ni (Mak.) : if he comes again

2. <u>in order to</u>

nani semu ni ka ima mata kaeritamaubeki (Uts.) : he will soon come back again for some reason (<u>or</u> to do something or other)

-MU TO SU   see TO SU

-MUZU   -MU -ZU 3. : comb. of aux. vbs. expressing will or intention

izuchi mo izuchi mo ashi no mukitaramu kata e inamuzu (Tak.) : he decided to go in each and every direction where his legs might carry him

ika de kaeramuzuramu (Mak.) : I wonder how I am going to get home

-N

<u>ombin</u> form of -MU

hitotsu hachisu no mi to naran (Hei.) : we shall be born [again] on the same lotus

otoko wa te uken (Mak.) : the man is going to keep his hand [in a game of <u>go</u>]

NA

1. pers. pron., 2nd pers. sing. : <u>you</u>, <u>thou</u>*

na koso wa otoko ni imaseba (Koj.) : since you are indeed a man

62

2. neg. impera. part. : <u>do not</u> (follows <u>shūshikei</u>)

kuchioshū omoikuzōru <u>na</u> (GM) : do not sink into help-less despondency

tauru <u>na</u> (Mak.) : do not fall over

3. interj. part. (follows <u>shūshikei</u>)

kimi to omouramu <u>na</u> (GM) : he must certainly realize who you are

ito sukitamaeri <u>na</u> (Mak.) : he's a real dandy, isn't he?

sokonau <u>na</u> (Mak.) : you'll damage it, you know

medetashi <u>na</u> (Mak.) : wasn't it splendid?

4. <u>mizenkei</u> of -NU 1. (follows <u>renyōkei</u>)

koto mo naku ware wa gaiserare<u>na</u>mashi (Tak.) : I might easily have been killed

5. optative part. (follows <u>mizenkei</u>)*

ie kika <u>na</u> (Man.) : I want to hear [the name of] your family

tanoshiku wo ara <u>na</u> (Man.) : let us be happy!

6. <u>ombin</u> form of NANI; NARI, NARU

<u>na</u>defu koto (Mak.) : what sort of thing?

yuku<u>na</u>meri (Mak.) : he seems to go

7. <u>ombin</u> form of NASHI, NAKI

kami<u>na</u>zuki (Mak.) : the month without gods (= the Tenth Month)

tanomoshige <u>na</u> no koto ya (Mak.) : that really does not make you sound very dependable

ito <u>na</u>ge nite (Mak.) : appearing not to have any leisure

NA (continued)

8. genitive case part.*

mi na soko (Man.) : at the bottom of the water

Minazuki (Mak.) : the watery month (= the Sixth Month)

9. stem of NASHI

shiranami (Shui) : the fact of not knowing

-NABA   -NA 4.   -BA la.

mikoto naritamainaba (GM) : if it devolves on the Prince

ushi ni narinaba ashikari namu (Mak.) : it certainly would not do [if I remained] until the Hour of the Ox

-NABAYA   -NA 5.   -BAYA

ikiusenabaya to omou (Mak.) : I wish that I could go and disappear for good

NABE NI

conj. phrase meaning together with, along with, while, as (follows rentaikei)

yamagawa no se no naru nabe ni (Man.) : together with the sound of the mountain stream

NADEFU   see NAJŌ

NADO

1. interr. adv. : why? what? (usually precedes rentaikei)

nado kaku shi mo omouramu (GM) : why should he think just that?

nado ka (Mak.) : what [are you saying]?

2. adv. part. expressing indefiniteness, vagueness, etc. : such as, for instance, and so on, to the effect; also used as a plur. suff. (as in hito nado = people)**

awaji ya nado hohoemite notamau (Tsutsu.) : smiling, he made a suggestion to the effect that she might have met...

mono ii nado su (Mak.) : they were talking

birōge no kuruma nado wa (Mak.) : a thing like a palm-leaf carriage

ame nado furu mo okashi (Mak.) : it is charming too when it rains

NADOTE (KA)   NADO 1.   -TE 1.   (KA 4.) : why? how? what?

nadote norisoite yukazaritsuramu (GM) : why do you suppose he went riding unaccompanied?

nadote tsukigoro mo mōdezu sugushitsuramu (Mak.) : how could I have stayed away from temples for so many months?

nadote ka makuru ni narazaramu (Mak.) : why should he not have lost?

NAGARA

conj. part. expressing temporal coincidence or concession : as, at the same time as, while, though (follows renyōkei or adj. stem)

kuinagara fumi wo mo yomikeri (Tsure.) : at the same time as eating, he read the letter

mi wa iyashinagara haha namu miko narikeru (Ise) : while he was of low rank, his mother was a princess

...koto to shirinagara (Mak.) : though I realized that...

NAJIKA

interr. adv. : why? (abbr. of NANI SHI NI KA)

najika wa on-mi wo oshimasetamaisaburaubeki (Hei.) : why should she be unwilling to sacrifice herself?

65

NAJŌ   NA 6.   -CHŌ : what sort of? why? something or other

   najō koto (Mak.) : what sort of thing?

   najō onna ga mannabumi wa yomu (MSN) : why should
   women read Chinese characters?

NAKARI   NAKU 1.   -ARI 1.

   ...koso saiwai nakarikere (GM) : it is indeed un-
   fortunate

   Miyako no uchi ni saru mono nakarikeru (Mak.) : there
   was not a single such person [left] in the capital

NAKARISHI   NAKARI   -SHI 3.

   sono go wa sata nakarishi wo (Hei.) : though he had no
   suggestions after that

NAKERE   NAKU 1.   -ARE 5.

   fune ni norite ariku hito bakari yuyushiki mono koso
   nakere (Mak.) : sailors are really the bravest people
   in the world

NAKEREDO(MO)   NAKU 1.   -ARE 5.   -DO(MO)

   unagashi nakeredomo (Hei.) : even though I did not
   urge them

NAKI

 rentaikei of NASHI

   katajikenaki mi-kokorobae no tagui naki wo tanomi nite
   (GM) : relying on your extraordinarily gracious nature

   mishi hito zo naki (Man.) : the person who saw it is
   dead

NAKU

 1. mizenkei and renyōkei of NASHI

   ma naku (Man.) : without pause

waza to asobi to wa naku tomo (GM) : though no special
entertainment had been arranged

2. NA 9. -KU 2a.

omowanaku (Man.) : the fact that I do not think

NAKU NI   NAKU 1.   NI 2. : without -ing, not - ing, though,
                  despite

matanaku ni (Man.) : without waiting

yuki dani kienaku ni (Kok.) : though the snow has not
even melted

shiranaku ni (Kok.) : though I do not know

-NAMASHI   -NA 4.   -MASHI 1.

ware gaiserarenamashi (Tak.) : I might have been killed

kotowari to oboshimesarenamashi (Mak.) : she would have
thought it reasonable

NAMERI   Na 6.   -MERI

komoru hito nameri (Mak.) : they seemed to be people
who had come for a retreat

kokoro ni makasu nameri to omou (Mak.) : you think you
can do as you please

ge ni sa nameri (Uts.) : it really seems so

NAMI   NA 9.   -MI 2.

shiranami (Shui) : the fact of not knowing

NAMU

1. emph. adv. part. (precedes rentaikei, or comes at end
of sentence)**

katachi yori wa kokoro namu masaritarikeru (Ise) : his
character (indeed) was superior to his looks

ashikari namu (Mak.) : that certainly would not do

NAMU (continued)

2. optative part. expressing hope or demand (cf. NA 5.)
(follows mizenkei)

chiru to iu koto wa narawazaranamu (Kok.) : oh, that
you may not learn how to scatter!

toku tachitamawanamu nado omoedo (Mak.) : though I
hoped he would leave quickly

3. NA 4. -MU : future emph. const., also expressing intention : will certainly, must surely (follows renyōkei)

sarubeki tsuide mo arinamu (GM) : things will surely
turn out as they should

ashiko ni komorinamu (GM) : I shall seclude myself
there

irinamu ya to omoite (Mak.) : intending (probably) to
enter

kaerinamu (Mak.) : let us go home!

4. mizenkei of nahen vb. -MU

yosoji ni taranu hodo nite shinamu koso meyasukarube-
kere (Tsure.) : it is certainly better to die before
one reaches the age of forty

NAMUCHI

pers. pron., 2nd pers. : you*

namuchira ga kaku makarinaba (Koj.) : would that you
had come thus!

NAN

1. same as NAMU

kimi ga kokoro mo ware ni tokenan (Kok.) : oh, that
your heart might melt towards me!

2. same as NANI

nan no kai ka wa arubeki (Hei.) : what good would it
do?

NANARI   NA 6.   -NARI

shirushiokikeru nanari (GM) : they do in fact record...

waga nanari to kikeba (Mak.) : as I heard [the bell] I
felt it was really for me

NANI

1. inter. pron. : what?

nani wo ka omowamu (Man.) : what shall I think?

2. interr. adv. : how? why?

harugasumi nani kakusuramu (Kok.) : why should the
spring mists hide...?

NANIGASHI

1. indef. adj. : a certain

nanigashi tera (GM) : a certain temple

Ariwara no nanigashi (Hei.) : Ariwara somebody-or-
other

2. pers. pron., 1st pers. : I

nanigashi ga mihabereba (Mak.) : because I am looking

NANI MO   NANI 1.   MO 1. : pron. phrase meaning anything,
            everything

tonoimono mo nani mo umorenagara (Mak.) : burying
bedding and all

NANI NI   NANI 1.   NI 1.

nani ni tsuketaru zo (Mak.) : why (lit. for what)
have they given it [that name]?

NANI SHI KA (WA)   NANI 2.   SHI 4.   KA(WA) : why? what for?

nani shi ka wa eshirazu to iishi (Mak.) : why did you
reply that you could not know?

69

NANI SHI NI   NANI 1. SHI 2. NI 1. : interr. adv. phrase
               meaning why? for what purpose?

    nani shi ni...kakaru ukime woba mirubeki (Hei.) : why
    should I have experienced such a painful thing?

NANI TO KA YA   NANI 1. TO 3a. KA 4. YA 1. : something
                 (someone) or other

    Mitsu nani to ka ya iu mono (Mak.) : a man called
    Mitsu...I cannot remember the rest of his name

NANI ZO

  same as NAN ZO

NANJI

  pers. pron., 2nd pers. sing. : you, thou (ombin form of
  NAMUCHI)

    nanji ga kubi (Hei.) : your head

NANJŌ

  same as NAJŌ

    nanjō koto ni sawari (Mak.) : something or other pre-
    vented me [from visiting you], and...

NAN ZO

  1. NAN 2. ZO 1. : interr. pron. : what (indeed)?

    nan zo to towasetamau (Uts.) : Their Excellencies
    asked what [had happened]

  2. NAN 2. ZO 2. : interr. adv. : how? why?

    nan zo kokorozashi wo togezaramu (Uji) : why will you
    not accomplish your aim?

NAO

  adv. : further, (still) more, yet, again; as usual, also,
  after all

    nao shibashi kokoromiyo (GM) : let us try a little
    longer

70

sora wa nao kasumi mo yarazu (Shinkokin) : the sky as
usual is not misty

NARA

mizenkei of NARI 1. and of NARU 2.-3.

inochi wo ushinau mono naraba (Hei.) : if we are going
to lose our lives anyhow

NARABA   NARA -BA la.

see NARA for example

NARAMU   NARA -MU

keosoroshū omowasuru naramu (GM) : His Excellency
seemed frightened

nanigoto naramu to (Mak.) : wondering what it might be

NARAZU   NARA -ZU

higoro no nasake mo ima wa nani narazu (Hei.) : the
friendship you have shown me all along now amounts to
nothing

kanarazu yoki hito narazu (Mak.) : certainly not being
people of high rank

NARE

1. izenkei of NARI 1. and of NARU 2.-3.

tsuyu koso aware nare (Tsure.) : the dew is indeed
moving

Uteikoku ga koto ni koso haberu nare (Mak.) : you must
be referring to Uteikoku

2. mizenkei and renyōkei of NARU 4.

mine no kasegi no chikaku naretaru ni tsukete mo
(Hoj.) : as the deer on the peaks become more and
more tame

71

NAREBA   NARE 1. -BA 1b.

kakitsuzukuru mo nakanaka nareba (Eiga) : since it
would take a long time to go into details (lit. to
continue writing)

atarashiki yutan nareba (Mak.) : since it was a new
oilcloth

NAREDO(MO)   NARE 1. -DO(MO)

hoshi yasurau keshiki naredo (Tsutsu.) : though the
priest looked as if he was resting

ito kiyoge naredo (Mak.) : though they were very
beautiful

NARE YA   NARE 1. YA 2. : const. used in poetry to denote
likeness or comparison

shio miteba irinuru iso no kusa nare ya (Man.) : like
the seaweed on the shore when the tide comes in

NARI

1. renyokei and shushikei of nari

(a) copula or affirmative vb. suff. (NI 3. -ARI 1a.)
(equiv. to modern de aru) : is, are (follows subst.,
uninfl. adj., or rentaikei)**

ume no hana ima sakari nari (Man.) : the plum
blossoms are now at their best

onna mo shite mimu tote suru nari (Tosa) : a woman too
will try her hand at it

ika naru hito narikemu (Tsure.) : what sort of a person can it have been?

(b) aux. vb. expressing report, seeming, appearance
(equiv. to modern so desu) : it is said that, I have
heard that, it appears that (follows shushikei, exc.
after rahen vbs. when it follows rentaikei, e.g. ku-
nari but arunari)

shizumarinunari (GM) : I hear that it has become
quiet

72

N.B. NARI 1a. and NARI 1b. are indistinguishable after (i) yodan vbs. (because their shūshikei and rentaikei forms are identical), (ii) rahen vbs. (because here NARI 1b. follows the rentaikei). E.g. yuku nari can mean both "he goes" and "I hear that he goes"; haberu nari can mean both "he serves" and "it appears that he serves." The context must decide.

2. renyōkei of NARU 2.-3.

mitsu ni naritamau toshi (GM) : the year in which she became two years old

nari takashi (GM) : you are being noisy

NARISHI   NARI -SHI 3.

ito omoi no hoka narishi koto nari (Hoj.) : it was a very unexpected thing

imijiku okashige narishi hito (Tsutsu.) : an extremely charming-looking man

NARU

1. rentaikei of NARI 1.

kiyoge naru otoko (Tsure.) : a handsome man

hi no ito uraraka naru ni (GM) : the sun being very bright

ika naru hito narikemu (Tsure.) : what sort of a person can it have been?

denjōbito jige naru mo (Mak.) : even people who were senior courtiers and gentlemen of the lower ranks

2. shūshikei and rentaikei of yodan vb. naru ("to become")

kimi ga yumi ni mo naramashi mono wo (Man.) : oh, that I might become your bow!

to oboshinaredo (GM) : though she thought that... (lit. it became a thought that...)

73

NARU (continued)

3. shūshikei and rentaikei of yodan vb. naru ("to cry,"
"to make a noise")

    mune tsubutsubu to naru kokochi su (GM) : he felt his
heart pounding heavily

4. shūshikei of shimonidan vb. naru ("to be accustomed")

    on-me naru (GM) : become accustomed to seeing

5. NI 1. -ARU 1.

    kitayama naru nanigashi tera (GM) : a certain temple
in the northern hills

    kono yo naru ma wa (Man.) : while we are in this world

    mae naru hito ni mo (Mak.) : to the woman who is in
front

NASA

1. NA 9. -SA 1.

    o-mae watari obotsukanasa (Mak.) : anxiety about what
was happening to Her Majesty

    ikeru kai nasa yo (Mak.) : oh, the pointlessness of
life!

2. mizenkei of NASU

    hitokoto wo kanarazu nasamu to omowaba (Tsure.) : if
you are determined to do one thing

NASARU

hon. yodan vb. : to do, make (= mizenkei of NASU -RU 2.)

    tatari nasaru na (Yam.) : pray do not incur a curse
(punishment)

NASHI

1. shūshikei of nashi, adj. predicating negation,
absence, death

<u>nashi</u> to kotaete (Kok.) : answering that I am not
there

2. <u>renyōkei</u> of NASU 1.

 higashi no kado wa yotsuashi ni <u>nashite</u> (Mak.) :
 having made the east gate into a four-post [structure]

NA...SO (NE) NA 2. SO 2. (NE 3.) : neg. impera. const.
      (the intervening vb. is in <u>renyōkei</u> exc. for
      <u>kahen</u> and <u>sahen</u> vbs., which are in <u>mizenkei</u>,
      e.g. na <u>kiki</u> so, but na <u>ko</u> so)

 koe <u>na</u> kikase <u>so</u> (Kok.) : do not let me hear your voice

 yuki <u>na</u> fumi <u>so ne</u> (Man.) : pray do not tread on the
 snow

 sa <u>na</u> se <u>so</u> (Mak.) : don't do that

NASU

1. hon. <u>sahen</u> vb. : <u>to do</u>, <u>make</u>, <u>accomplish</u>, <u>achieve</u>,
<u>effect</u>

 higashi no kado wa yotsuashi ni <u>nashite</u> (Mak.) : the
 east gate had been made into a four-post [structure]

 <u>nasu</u> koto nakute (Zoku Kokin Waka Shū) : there being
 nothing to do

2. hon. aux. <u>sahen</u> vb. (follows <u>renyōkei</u>)

 ...to omoi<u>nashi</u>tamau ni (GM) : His Excellency, thinking that...

NAZO

same as NADO 1.

 kimi nakuba <u>nazo</u> mi yosowamu (Man.) : if you are not
 there, why should I adorn myself?

NE

1. <u>meireikei</u> of -NU 1. (follows <u>renyōkei</u>)
 mi-kōshi mairi<u>ne</u> (GM) : close the lattice
 netamai<u>ne</u> (Mak.) : go to sleep

NE (continued)

2. izenkei of -ZU 1. (follows mizenkei)

fukiiretaru koso arakaritsuru kaze no shiwaza to mo
oboene (Mak.) : I certainly do not think it was the
strong wind that blew them in

tori ni shi araneba (Man.) : since I am (certainly) not
a bird

3. desid., mild impera., or hortative part. (follows
mizenkei)*

na norasane (Man.) : pray tell me your name

-NEBA   -NE 2.   -BA 1b.

sawarite eiraneba (Mak.) : since it got blocked and
could not enter

-NEDO(MO)   -NE 2.   -DO(MO)

sue made wa aranedomo (Mak.) : though it does not go
all the way

chiisō wa aranedo (Mak.) : though she was not small

NE KA SHI   NE 1.   KA SHI : mild impera. or hortative comb.
of parts.

saraba saraba haya ite owashimashine ka shi (Uts.) :
well well, then, by all means come and stay

toku furiyamine ka shi to koso oboyure (Mak.) : I can
only wish that it would stop raining soon

NI

1. dative, instrumental, or locative case part. : in, on,
at, to, by, for

Suruga no Kuni ni annaru yama no itadaki ni moteyuku-
beki yoshi (Tak.) : that I should carry it to the top
of the mountain that is said to be in Suruga
Province

hito ni anazuraruru mono (Mak.) : things despised by
people

akatsuki ni iku tote (Mak.) : hearing that she was
going to leave at dawn

2. coordinating conj. part. with extended use as concessive, cond., causal, etc. : along with, together with, and,
-ing, when, while, whereas, if, although, since, because
(follows rentaikei)

shika no tatazumiariku mo mezurashiku mitamau ni (GM) :
admiring the deer as they walked along and stopped

hito no ushiromi to tanomikikoemu ni (GM) : whereas I
rely on you as a (person's) guardian

mina netaru ni (Mak.) : since everyone was asleep

kokorozashi aru ni wa eseji (Mak.) : if he had any
sincere feeling, he could probably not do it

nao obotsukanaki ni (Mak.) : since I was still uncertain

3. conj. part. (functioning as renyōkei of NARI 1.; equiv.
to modern de)

imijū aware ni okashikere (Mak.) : it is extremely
moving and charming

kumorigachi ni haberumeri (GM) : it looks cloudy

kore wa tatsu no shiwaza ni koso arikere (Tak.) : it is
the dragon and none other that has done this

kurai koso nao medetaki mono ni wa are (Mak.) : rank
is, after all, a most splendid thing

4. renyōkei of -NU 1. (follows renyōkei)

fujinami sakinikeri (Kok.) : the wistaria have
blossomed in waves

mairazu nariniki (Yam.) : it turned out that I could
not go

5. desid. part. (follows mizenkei)*

nari wo shimasani (Man.) : please see to your duties

NI (continued)

6. intensifying part. (follows renyōkei)

yo wa tada ake ni aku (GM) : the night is indeed coming to an end quickly

namida wo tada otoshi ni otosu (Mak.) : he cried and cried miserably

machi ni ka matamu (Man.) : shall I keep waiting for him?

hori ni horite (Mak.) : digging away busily

tada ori ni orite tataeru kurumadomo wo tada noke ni nokesasete (Mak.) : they leapt off [their horses] and lost no time in making the carriages move out of the way

7. adv. part.

(a) forming adv. phrases from subst. forms

tairaka ni mōdetsukitaru (Mak.) : (the fact of) his returning safely

(b) indicating the condition into which something or someone is changed

kimi ga yumi ni mo naramashi (Man.) : would that I might become your spear!

hodo naku mare ni narite (Tsure.) : soon becoming scarce

8. renyōkei of -ZU 1. (follows mizenkei)*

yukue wo shirani (Man.) : not knowing the way

9. same as no yō ni = "in the manner of," "as if"

kotoba ni mi-tezukara kakasetamaishi (Mak.) : she had written on it with her own hand as though it were an ordinary sentence

mezamashiki mono ni otoshisonemitamau (GM) : they regarded her with scorn and jealousy as (in the manner of) a vexatious person

10. conj. part. : in order to, for the purpose of (precedes renyōkei of certain vbs. esp. vbs. of motion)

yu ni orite (GM) : going down in order to perform his
ablutions

nani shi ni kakaru mono ni tsukawaruru zo (Mak.) : why
(lit. in order to do what) are you employed by such a
person?

hito wo nose ni ikitaru (Mak.) : I went to fetch someone in my carriage

NI ARAZU   NI 3.   ARA 2.   -ZU 1.

moto no mizu ni arazu (Hoj.) : it is not the same
water

hiku ni wa arazu (Mak.) : no one was playing [the
lute]

NI ARI

same as NARI 1. (= NI 3.   ARI 1a.)

moshi oya nakute yo no naka kataho ni aritomo (GM) :
even though one may be handicapped by having no
parents

NI ARITE   NI 3.   ARI 1.   -TE 1.

on-monogatari shimeyaka ni arite yo ni irite (GM) : the
things he was relating were of a quiet intimacy, and he
went on talking into the night

NI KA

1. NI 3. KA 4. comb. of parts. indicating probability or
conjecture (cf. modern ka shira) (follows rentaikei)

ika ni narikeru ni ka (Hoj.) : I wonder what became of
them

ika ni obosu ni ka (Mak.) : I do not know what [Her
Majesty] thought about it

izure wo yoki ashiki to wa shiru ni ka aramu (Mak.) :
how am I to know which is good and which is bad?

NI KA (continued)

2. NI 1.   KA 4.

izure no on-toki ni ka (GM) : during some reign or
other

-NIKERI   -NI 4.   -KERI

kōbai...irozukinikeri (GM) : the plum blossoms were
(or had become) colourful

hisashū narinikeru (Mak.) : a long time had passed

-NIKI   -NI 4.   -KI 3.

moto no sama ni nariniki (Mak.) : he returned to his
former state

mairazu nariniki (Yam.) : it turned out that I could
not go

NI MO ARE...NI MO ARE   NI 3. MO 1. ARE 3. : whether...or

mukashi arikeru koto ni mo are ima kikoshimeshi yo ni
iikeru koto ni mo are (Mak.) : whether something in the
past or some recent event that he has heard people
discuss

-NISHI   -NI 4.   -SHI 3.

owashinishi wo (Mak.) : the gentlemen left, and...

suginishi kata (Mak.) : the time that passed

-NISHIGANA   see -SHIGANA

-NISHIKA   -NI 4.   -SHIKA 1.

...koso...odorokarenishika (Mak.) : we were certainly
surprised

Saishō ni naritamainishikaba (Mak.) : because His
Excellency became an Imperial Adviser

NI SHITE

same as NI ARITE

kentōshi <u>ni shite</u> (Hei.) : being an envoy to China

-NITARI   -NI 4.   -TARI 1.

koe mina karewatari<u>nitari</u> (GM) : their voices had all become completely h<u>oarse</u>

wabishū iware<u>nitari</u> (Mak.) : it grieves him to have been addressed [like that]

NITE

1. instrumental or locative case part. (contr. of NI 1. -ARI 1. -TE 1.) : <u>by</u>, <u>with</u>, <u>at</u>, <u>in</u>

sebaki tokoro <u>nite</u> hi <u>nite</u> monoiri nado shite (Tsure.): cooking food (<u>lit.</u> making with fire) in a small place

kuruma <u>nite</u> mo kachi <u>nite</u> mo (Mak.) : both in a carriage and on foot

2. NI 3. -TE 1. : conj. part. (equiv. to modern <u>de atte</u>) (follows subst., uninfl. adj., or <u>rentaikei</u>)

ajiki naki susabi <u>nite</u> (Tsure.) : being an idle distraction

medetaki on-ikioi <u>nite</u> (GM) : having (<u>or</u> being of) impressive power

nao suru koto <u>nite</u> arishi (Tsure.) : it was still being done

NITE ARI

same as NARI 1a.

Hidan no Ōidono no kata no hito shiru suji <u>nite ari</u> (Mak.) : she is on close terms with people <u>of the</u> Minister of the Left's faction

ani mo Kyō nite hōshi <u>nite ari</u> (Kage.) : his brother was (also) a cleric in <u>the capital</u>

81

NI TSUKETE (MO or WA)

phrase meaning <u>as</u>, <u>when</u>, <u>in connexion with</u>, <u>in proportion to</u>

Kyō no narai naniwaza ni tsukete mo mina moto inaka wo koso tanomeru ni (Hoj.) : whereas the capital has always been basically dependent on the countryside in all respects

hodohodo <u>ni tsukete wa</u> (Mak.) : befitting (<u>or</u> in proportion to) his rank

wasuresasetamau ni tsukete mo mi mo otoroenuru hodo omoishirarete (Hei.) : knowing how much my appearance must have deteriorated from the way you have forgotten me.

NI YA

same as NI KA

omoianazuritaru <u>ni ya</u> arikemu (Mak.) : would they have looked down on them?

mada fukakaraneba <u>ni ya</u> (GM) : perhaps because it was not yet late

sayō no koto ni tsukaetatematsuru hito mo naki <u>ni ya</u> (Hei.) : is there no one who could do such a thing for her?

makoto <u>ni ya</u> aramu (Mak.) : I wonder whether it is true

rei no on-asobi <u>ni ya</u> aramu to oshihakarite (GM) : imagining that there would be the usual entertainment

NO

1. possessive case part.

yūbi no sashite yama <u>no</u> ha ito chikō naritaru ni (Mak.) : when the evening sun shines and approaches very close to the edge of the hills

2. nominative case part. (esp. in subordinate clauses)

yūbi <u>no</u> sashite (Mak.) : the evening sun shines

hito <u>no</u> motekitaru (Mak.) : people bring

3. same as GA 5.

inishie no wa aware naru koto ōkari (Tsure.) : there
are many moving things among the ancient [writings]

NŌ

ombin form of NAKU

kokochi nō sashisugushite (GM) : she pushes herself
forward heedlessly

NOMI

1. adv. : only

tada nami no shiroki nomi zo miyuru (Tosa) : one could
see only the white of the waves

2. intensifying adv. meaning most, very

on-mune nomi tsuto futagarite (GM) : being suddenly
overcome by the most [poignant] emotion

NOTAMAU

hon. yodan vb. : to speak, say

nanigoto wo ka notamawamu (Tak.) : what will Your
Highness say?

sa notamawaba (Mak.) : if you speak like that, Madam...

-NU

1. shūshikei of -nu, affirmative, emph., or past nahen vb.
suff. (generally affixed to intransitive vbs.) : ended by
-ing, at last -, etc., but ** (follows renyōkei)

mono wo nomi kuite yo fukenu (Tosa) : did nothing but
eat until night (finally) fell

mi-ko sae umaretamainu (GM) : an (honourable) child
has been born

Kurōdo ni narinu (Mak.) : he became a Chamberlain

idenu (Mak.) : I left

-NU (continued)

2. rentaikei of -ZU 1. (follows mizenkei)

yokaranu koto nari (Tsure.) : it is not a good thing

miredo akanu Yoshino no kawa (Man.) : Yoshino River, on which I never tire of gazing

-NUBESHI   -NU 1.   -BESHI : (certainly) will have

yo fukehaberinubeshi (GM) : the night will have grown late

arinubeki tokoro wo toraete (Mak.) : grasping part [of the material] where there is bound to be [a threaded needle]

-NURAMU   -NU 1.   -RAMU 1.

ima wa mina noritamainuramu to koso omoitsure (Mak.) : I really thought that everyone must have got into a carriage by now

ne no toki nado ni mo narinuramu (Mak.) : it would appear to be about midnight (lit. it has evidently become about the Hour of the Rat)

-NURE

1. izenkei of -NU 1.

aki no hatsukaze fukinureba (Hei.) : once the first autumn winds had blown

chikō kinureba (Mak.) : when we had come near

2. izenkei of nahen vbs. and of shimonidan vbs. ending in -nu

jishite inureba (Uts.) : when he had paid his respects and left

-NURU

rentaikei of -NU 1.

izukata e ka makarinuru (GM) : where can he have gone (or ended by going)?

84

Daijin nado ni narinuru wa (Mak.) : [now] that he has become a Great Minister

O

1. hon. pref. (abbr. of ON-)

   o-mae ni meshiidete (Uts.) : summoning him into the Presence

2. see WO

Ō

1. ombin form of -o,a (adj. stem) -KU 1.

   norō tomo (Mak.) : though it is slow

   chikō kinureba (Mak.) : when we had come near

2. ombin form of -au (vb. ending)

   toridori ni tamō (GM) : His Excellency gave each of them

OBOSHIMESU

same as OBOSU

   goranjihatemu to oboshimesu ni (GM) : His Excellency decided to see things through and...

   tada wakaki hito wo nomi oboshimeshite (Mak.) : liking only young people

   nanigoto wo oboshimesuramu (Mak.) : what can you have to worry about

OBOSU

hon. yodan vb. : to think, consider, understand; love, esteem, worry about

   obosuramu koto (Tak.) : what His Excellency must be thinking

85

OI

interj. : <u>oh</u>! <u>hullo</u>!

<u>oi</u> kono kimi ni koso (Mak.) : oh, it's that lord!

<u>oi</u> <u>oi</u> sanari sanari (Eiga) : oh, yes, yes!

OMAE

pers. pron., 2nd pers. sing. : <u>you</u>, <u>thou</u>

ore wa <u>omae</u> ni kashikō ōseraruru ni wa arazu (Mak.) :
there was nothing clever about your saying that

ŌMI-

hon. pref. used of emperors and gods

<u>ōmi</u>-koto (Shoku) : the august word

OMOTO

1. pers. pron., 2nd pers. : <u>you</u> (of women)

<u>omoto</u> ni kuwasetatematsuramu tote (Uts.) : intending
to serve you (<u>lit</u>. cause you to eat) [the fish]

2. subst. : <u>personal attendant to the emperor</u>

jōrō no <u>omoto</u> nado sōrō (Uts.) : noblewomen and other
ladies were in attendance

ON-

hon. pref.**

kono <u>on</u>-michi (Mak.) : this path of yours

<u>on</u>-kudamono (Mak.) : fruit

ONORE

reflexive or pers. pron., 1st, 2nd, and 3rd pers. (dis-
respectful when used of the 2nd and 3rd pers.)

<u>onore</u> woba shirazaru nari (Tsure.) : he does not know
me

<u>onore</u> wa tenjō yori kitaritamaishi hito no on-kodomo
<u>nari</u> (Uts.) : I am the child of one who came down from
heaven

<u>onore</u> wa magamagashikarikeru kokoro mochitaru mono ka
na (Uji) : this fellow certainly has an unpleasant
nature, doesn't he?

ORE

same as ONORE

<u>ore</u> yo kayatsu yo (Mak.) : oh, you wretched creature!

<u>ore</u> wa nanigoto iu zo (Uji): how dare you say such a
thing? (<u>lit</u>. what have you said?)

<u>orera</u> shiranu ni (Sanuki Tenji Nikki) : although we
(humble creatures) did not know it

ORI

<u>renyōkei</u> and <u>shūshikei</u> of <u>ori</u>, <u>rahen</u> vb. : <u>to exist</u>, <u>be</u>,
<u>continue in a given condition</u>

hito sawa ni irioritomo (Koj.) : though he entered the
swamp (and stayed there)

nenjiirite <u>ori</u> (GM) : he continued praying fervently

uta ni hazurete wa <u>oru</u> (Mak.) : you are not joining in
this evening's poetry

-ŌTE   see -AUTE

OWASU

1. hon. <u>shimonidan</u> and <u>yodan</u> vb. : <u>to be</u>, <u>have</u>, <u>come</u>,
<u>stand</u>, <u>arrive</u>, <u>attend</u>, <u>leave</u>

<u>owashinishi</u> (Mak.) : the gentlemen returned home

<u>owasaneba</u> (GM) : because His Highness had not come

Sanjō no Miya ni <u>owashimasu</u> koro (Mak.) : when Her
Majesty was residing in the Palace of the Third Ward

OWASU 1. (continued)

    miya waroku <u>owashima</u>sazu (MSN) : the Princess is of
high birth

    ito tsukizukishū okashūte <u>owasu</u> (Mak.) : he [the
Captain] was most appropriately and pleasantly
accoutred

2. hon. aux. vb. (follows <u>renyōkei</u>) (<u>shimonidan</u> and <u>yodan</u>)

    Chūgū no kaku so<u>iowasu</u>ru ni mi-kokoro okarete (GM) :
noticing that the Empress thus (deigned to) accompany...

    nado kaku hakarawase<u>owashi</u>masu (Mak.) : how could Your
Majesty deceive me like that?

    kaesugaesu zu shite <u>owasu</u>ru wa (Mak.) : the fact that
the gentleman recited it over and over

RA

1. exclam. part.*

    tsuma wo <u>ra</u> okite <u>ra</u> mo kinu (Man.) : I have (indeed)
come leaving behind (indeed) my wife

2. plur. suff.

    otome<u>ra</u> (Man.) : maidens

-RAE

<u>mizenkei</u> and <u>renyōkei</u> of -RAYU 1.

    ne<u>rae</u>nu ni (Man.) : being unable to sleep

-RAKU   see -KU 2.

-RAME

1. <u>izenkei</u> of -RAMU 1.

    mizukara imiji to omou<u>rame</u>do ito kuchioshi (Tsure.) :
although they seem to be pleased with themselves,
actually they are worthless

ashiko made mo yukitsukazaruramedo (Mak.) : even
though it may not have reached its destination

2. mizenkei of yodan or rahen vb. ending in -ru -ME

ware koso kono kawari mo tsukōmatsurame (Eiga) : I
myself shall perform the office in her place

-RAMU

1. shūshikei and rentaikei of -ramu, aux. yodan vb. expressing doubt, seeming, conjecture, probability (follows
shūshikei exc. after rahen vbs. when it follows rentaikei,
e.g. taburamu but haberuramu)

hito ni iuramu koto wo maneburamu (Mak.) : they
evidently imitate what people say

suzushiki kaze ya fukuramu (Kok.) : a cool wind must
be blowing

2. mizenkei of yodan or rahen vb. ending in -ru -MU

kokoro shireramu hito (Gosen) : a person who would
know my feelings

kore ni itoguchi tōshite tamawaramu (Mak.) : you will
kindly pass a thread through this

-RAN

contr. of -RAMU 1.

ōgi wo isaserarubyō ya sōroran (Hei.) : it would probably be best, Excellency, to order that the fan be
shot down

-RARE

1. mizenkei and renyōkei of -RARU 1.

ne mo nerarezu (Sara.) : I could not sleep a wink

ueraretarikeru botan (Mak.) : the peonies that have
been planted

-RARE (continued)

2. mizenkei of yodan or rahen vb. ending in -ru -RE 1.

mino toraretaru kokochi shite (Mak.) : feeling that my
straw coat had been taken from me

-RARU

1. shūshikei of -raru, passive, potential, reflexive, and
hon. vb. suff. (shimonidan) (follows mizenkei of all exc.
yodan, nahen, and rahen vbs.; cf. -RU 2.)

yorozu no koto itawararu (Uji) : he graciously cared
for him in different ways

2. mizenkei of yodan or rahen vb. ending in -ru -RU 2.

mino toraru (Mak.) : to have one's straw coat taken

-RARURE

1. izenkei of -RARU 1.

oserarureba (Mak.) : when His Majesty said...

hitoya no on-monogatari koso omoiiderarure (Akazome
Shū) : His Excellency called to mind the (very) story
of what happened one night

2. mizenkei of yodan or rahen vb. ending in -ru -RURE 2.

mitarikemu koso omoiyararure (Mak.) : one can certainly
imagine what he must have felt when he saw it

-RARURU

1. rentaikei of -RARU 1.

to namu ōseraruru (Mak.) : she said that...

kore ni oshieraruru mo okashi (Mak.) : it was amusing
to have been instructed by him

2. mizenkei of yodan or rahen vb. ending in -ru -RURU 2.

hito ni anazuraruru mono (Mak.) : things that are
despised by people

-RASHI

shūshikei of -rashi, aux. shikukatsuyō adj. expressing
doubt, probability, seeming : may be, seem to, probably
will, -ish, -like (follows shūshikei exc. after rahen vbs.
when it follows rentaikei, e.g. taburashi but orurashi;
also follows subst. or adj. stem)

    kari wa komurashi (Kok.) : it looks as if the geese
    will be coming

    otomego mo kamisabinurashi (GM) : the maiden seemed old-
    fashioned

-RASHIKI

rentaikei of -RASHI

    utsusemi mo tsuma wo arasourashiki (Man.) : even
    cicadas appear to fight for their wives (i.e. to
    engage in contests to decide who will get a certain
    female)

-RAYU

1. same as -RARU 1. (follows mizenkei)*

    (N.B. used mainly after neru ("to sleep") (see -RAE)
    and in potential sense)

2. mizenkei of yodan or rahen vb. ending in -ru -YU 2.

    surayu na (Man.) : let it not be rubbed!

-RE

1. mizenkei and renyōkei of -RU 2. (follows mizenkei)

    koshi namu ugokarenu (Tak.) : he was (completely) un-
    able to move his hips

    kuruma ni oshihishigaretaru (Mak.) : it was crushed by
    the carriage

2. mizenkei and renyōkei of shimonidan vb. ending in -ru

    himugashi ni nagaresaru (Tsure.) : it flows away to
    the east

-RE (continued)

3. <u>izenkei</u> and <u>meireikei</u> of <u>yodan</u> vb. ending in -<u>ru</u>

haru no yuki fureba (Kok.) : since there has been a
spring snowfall

-RI   see -ERI

-RU

1. <u>shūshikei</u> of certain vbs.

yo ni tōzakaru hodo wo shiru (Hoj.) : I realize how
remote I have become from people

2. <u>shimonidan</u> suff. with same meaning as -RARU 1. (follows <u>mizenkei</u> of <u>yodan</u>, <u>nahen</u>, and <u>rahen</u> vbs.)

netaru ashi wo kitsune ni kuwaru (Tsure.) : had his
foot eaten by a fox while he was asleep

-RURE

1. <u>izenkei</u> of <u>shimonidan</u> vb. ending in -<u>ru</u>

kokorozashi mo arawarure namu (Hei.) : his intentions
were probably apparent

2. <u>izenkei</u> of -RU 2. (follows <u>mizenkei</u>)

iotosarure (Hei.) : was brought down by an arrow

yarawaruredo (Mak.) : even though he is chased away

-RURU

1. <u>rentaikei</u> of <u>shimonidan</u> and <u>kaminidan</u> vbs. ending in
-<u>ru</u>

tsuki zo nagaruru (Kok.) : the moon (indeed) floats

kururu ma wa (Goshui) : when evening comes

oruru ka (Mak.) : are you going down?

2. **rentaikei** of -RU 2. (follows **mizenkei**)

hito ni anazuraruru mono (Mak.) : things that people despise

SA

1. subst. suff. (usually forming abstract nouns) follows adj. stem or **shūshikei** or -GE)

kaerusa ni (Man.) : on my return

ninjō no kokoroyogesa (Mak.) : the pleased look of the director

sabushisa (Man.) : helplessness

hito no monoiisaganasa yo (GM) : oh, the spitefulness of people!

2. adv. : **so, thus**

sa to wa nakute (GM) : not being thus

sa koso yo wo itou (Hei.) : to hate the world so

3. pers. pron., 3rd pers. : **he**

sa ga kami wo torite (Tak.) : taking his hair

SABA   SA 2. -A (abbr. of ARA) -BA la.

saba yokanari (Mak.) : in that case it is all right

SA BAKARI   SA 2. BAKARI : **to that extent, so much**

sa bakari kataraitsuru ga (Tak.) : the one who persuaded this many [people]

sa bakari shitaitsuru hitobito (Mak.) : the people who had been longing so keenly [to accompany us]

SABURAU

shūshikei and **rentaikei** of **saburau**

93

SABURAU (continued)

1. humble and polite yodan vb. : to be (in attendance), have; go, come, visit

   sono kuni no fukayama ni saburau (Uji) : I was deep in the mountains of that province (Your Lordship)

   Ue no omae ni Inakaeji to iu on-fue no saburau nari (Mak.) : His Majesty had a flute called Inakaeji

   saburawamu ni wa ikaga (Mak.) : may I come in?

   kanarazu saburaubeki mono (Mak.) : someone who should certainly be in attendance

   makoto ni ya saburauramu (Mak.) : will that really happen, Your Majesty?

   imijū namu saburaitsuru (Mak.) : it was really superb, Your Majesty

2. polite and humble aux. vb. (follows renyōkei)

   yomo nogashimairasesaburawaji (Hei.) : we could scarcely make our escape, Sir

   karai me wo misaburaitsuru (Mak.) : a terrible thing has happened to me

SAE

emph. adv. part. : in addition to, as well as, also, even**

   mitatematsuru hito sae (GM) : even onlookers

   mi sae hana sae sono ha sae e ni (Man.) : on its fruit, on its flowers, and on its leaves

SAFURAU   see SABURAU

SAMO

adv.

1. just like, as, such a, in that way, so

mada samo sadamerarezarumeri (Uts.) : it still does not appear to have been decided in that way

samo arazu (Mak.) : no (lit. it is not thus)

2. indeed, truly

okina samo iwaretari (Tak.) : the old man truly said...

SARADE   SA 2. -ARA 2. -DE

sarade da ni ayashiki hodo no yūgure (Goshui) : an evening that would have been strange even without that happening

sarade higoro mi miezu (Mak.) : [if,] on the other hand, I had not seen him for many days...

SARE

1. mizenkei of yodan vb. ending in -su -RE 1.

iro yurusaretaru wa (MSN) : those who were allowed to wear the [special] colours

2. izenkei of SARI 1. and of SARU 2.

saredo tokaku iu kai nakute (Hoj.) : their complaints, however, did them no good

3. SHI 4. -ARE 3.

Ōkimi no mikoto ni sareba (Man.) : since this is (indeed) what Her Ladyship ordered

4. abbr. of SE 2. -RARE 1.

isogasaretamaite (GM) : the Emperor hastened [his abdication]

SARI

1. SA 2. -ARI 1.

sarinubeki hima mo ya (GM) : a time that should truly have been

SARI (continued)

2. SHI 4. -ARI 1.

Ōkimi no mikoto ni sareba (Man.) : since it is (indeed)
Her Ladyship's instruction

3. renyōkei of SARU 2.

tokoro sarikikoemu (GM) : I shall yield my place

SARI TOMO   SARI 1. TOMO 1.

sari tomo oni nado mo wa woba miyurushitemu (GM) : will
the devils nevertheless let me go unscathed?

sari tomo hito ni wa otoritamawaji (GM) : he was nevertheless (probably) not inferior to others

SARI TOTE   SARI 1. TOTE 2.

sari tote ware woba ikaga to omoitaru kewai (Mak.) : a
sign, nevertheless, of how he regarded me

SARU

1. rentaikei of SARI 1. : such a

saru waza suru fune mo nashi (Tak.) : there was no boat
that could be used for such a task

2. shūshikei and rentaikei of yodan vb. saru ("to leave")

yamai sarubeki tokoro (GM) : a place where he could
avoid illness

SASE

1. mizenkei and renyōkei of -SASU

hito ni shikarubeki furumai wa saseji (GM) : will not
allow people to behave in that way

Miya no idesasetamau ni (Mak.) : when Her Majesty
proceeded

2. mizenkei of yodan vb. ending in -su -SE 2.

96

hata sasasetarikeru wa (Hei.) : the ones who ordered
the flag to be raised

Dono no kakusasetamaeru nameri (Mak.) : it must have
been His Excellency who ordered them to [do it]
secretly

3. abbr. of SE 1. -SASE 1.

tada sode wo toraete tōzai wo sasezu (Hei.) : just
clung to my sleeve without making anyone show me the
way

sono koto sasemu to su (Mak.) : I intend to order this
to be done

SASHI -

same as MOTE-

ito chikaku sashiayumi (Mak.) : walking (or forcing
their way) extremely close

SA SHI MO   SA 2.   SHI 4.   MO 3. : to such an extent
               (emph.)

sa shi mo on-itōshimi fukō koso sōraishi ni (Hei.) :
though you loved me so deeply (or all that much)

-SASU

shūshikei of -sasu, causative and hon. shimonidan vb.
suff. (follows mizenkei of all exc. yodan, nahen, and
rahen vbs.; cf. -SU 2.)

hito irete annai sesasu (GM) : he sent for a messenger
and ordered them to be brought in

Mikado no on-toshi nebisasetamainuredo (GM) : although
His Majesty was no longer young

-SASURE

1. izenkei of -SASU

hitodomo idashimotomesasuredo (Mak.) : though someone
was dispatched to look for it (or though I sent people
out in search)

-SASURE 1. (continued)

Ben no Omoto ni tsutaesasureba (Mak.) : when I told Ben no Omoto to transmit it

2. mizenkei of yodan vb. ending in -su -SURE 1.

ōyake ni kono yoshi wo mōsasureba (Uts.) : since he has expressed this in public

-SASURU

1. rentaikei of -SASU

momiji sesasuru aki wa kinikeri (Goshui) : autumn, which makes the leaves turn crimson, is here

2. mizenkei of yodan vb. ending in -su -SURU

SATE

1. SA 2. -ARI 1. -TE 1. : conj. meaning being thus, this being the case, this having been the case, with extended uses of after, the rest, the others

sate wa imijiku koso to oboeshika (Tsure.) : this being the case, I was certainly delighted

sate no hitobito wa (GM) : as for the other people

ika bakari naru kokochi nite sate miruramu (Mak.) : what would one feel if one saw it in such a situation (or under such circumstances)

sate koso nanji wo tsukawashitare (Hei.) : just because she was that kind of person, she sent you

2. continuative adv. meaning well, now, then

sate Kaguyahime (Tak.) : at this point Kaguyahime...

SE

1. mizenkei of SU 1., 3.

monogatari nado sesasetamau (GM) : he gave instructions that romances and other writings be made

ei mo sezu (iroha) : I shall not be fuddled any more

98

2. mizenkei and renyōkei of -SU 2.

arisama wo towasetamau (GM) : His Majesty inquired about the particulars

to iwasetamau (GM) : he told [her] to say that...

uchinakasetamau (Mak.) : His Excellency wept (copiously)

3. mizenkei of -KI 3.

yo no naka ni taete sakura no nakariseba (Kok.) : if cherry blossoms had never existed in the world

itsuwari no naki yo nariseba (Kok.) : if this were a world without lies

4. mizenkei and renyōkei of shimonidan vb. ending in -su and mizenkei of sahen vb.

tada tsukisenu mono wa namida nari (Hei.) : the only thing you cannot use up is tears

5. izenkei and meireikei of yodan vb. ending in -su

onokodomo meseba (Mak.) : having summoned some attendants

-SEBA

1. -SE 3. BA la.

sakura no nakariseba (Kok.) : if there were no cherry blossoms

kami nakariseba (Mak.) : if there were no god

2. -SE 1.-2. -BA la.

tsuyu araku mo seba (Mak.) : in case of (lit. if there was) the slightest roughness

SEDE   SE 1.-2. -DE

oki mo sezu ne mo sede yo wo akashite wa (Ise) : waited until daybreak without getting up but without going to sleep either

SEDE (continued)

katatoki arubeki kokochi mo sede (Mak.) : not feeling
that I can go on living for another moment (or feeling
that I cannot go on living for another moment)

SEJI   SE 1. -JI 1.

kokorozashi aru ni wa eseji (Mak.) : he could probably
not [behave like that] if he had any sincere feelings
[for me]

yuzuke dani kuwaseji (Mak.) : I should not give him
even [a bowl of] watered rice

SEMASHI   SE 1.-2. -MASHI 1.

fumi to iu koto nakaramashikaba ika ni ibuseku kure-
futagaru kokochi semashi (Mak.) : if there were no such
things as letters, how sad and gloomy I should feel!

SEMU   SE 1.-2. -MU

ikaga wa semu (Mak.) : what could we do about it?

medetashi to kikasemu to omoikereba (Mak.) : when she
was intending to say something impressive

meshite mawasemu (Mak.) : I shall summon them and tell
them to dance

-SERARU   -SE 2. -RARU : causative passive suff.

ōgi wo isaserarubyō ya sōrōran (Hei.) : it would probably be best, Excellency, to order that the fan be
shot down

-SESASE

1. -SE 2. -SASE 1.

kakasesasetamau (Mak.) : Her Ladyship makes her write

2. -SE 1. -SASE 1.

to keisesasetamae (Mak.) : tell [one of the Empress's
ladies-in-waiting] to say to Her Majesty...

-SESHI   -SE 2.   -SHI 3.

ika ni kaku wa nusumaseshi zo (Mak.) : how could you
let them be stolen like that?

SESHIKA   SE 4.   -SHIKA 1.   (see KI 3.)

kano In no Betō owaseshikaba (Mak.) : since he was the
Director of the [late] Emperor's household

SESHIMU   SE 1.-2.   -SHIMU

nani yue ni ka nyōgo sō seshimetamaikemu (Uts.) : why
do you suppose the lady-in-waiting acted like that?

SEYO

meireikei of SU

kawaki dani seyo (Kok.) : if only it would become dry

monogatari mo seyo mukashimonogatari mo seyo (Mak.) :
whether one is talking about recent events or discus-
sing something from the past (i.e. be it this or be
it that)

SEZU   SE 1.-2.   -ZU

mae naru hito ni mo torasezu (Mak.) : he does not give
(lit. cause to take) it to the lady who is in front of
him

SHI

1. (a) shūshikei of kukatsuyō adj. (follows adj. stem)

ito ushirometashi (Mak.) : it makes me very uneasy

(b) stem ending and shūshikei of shikukatsuyō adj.

ito wabishi (Tsure.) : it is quite unbearable

anazurawashiku (Mak.) : scornfully

2. renyōkei of SU 1., 3.

iritatanu sama shitaru (Tsure.) : to give the impression of not being too conversant

101

SHI (continued)

tsune ni owashite monogatari shi (Mak.) : His Excellency was always coming to chat [with me], and...

3. rentaikei of -KI 3. (follows renyōkei, but see -KI 3.
for exceptions)

yama e noborishi wa (Tsure.) : to have gone up into
the mountains

hito no homeshi koto (Mak.) : things people have said
in praise

mijikaku mieshi wo (Mak.) : they looked short

4. emph. or interj. part. (used chiefly in poetry, in
conditional protasis, and in the comb. KA SHI)

sakura shi kokoro araba (Kok.) : if cherry blossoms
only had feelings

amata shi areba (Mak.) : since there are so many

nado kaku shi mo omouramu (GM) : why should he think
just that?

seki shi masashiki mono naraba (Koj.) : if the barrier
is a true [reliable] thing

SHIGA   see GA 4.

-SHIGANA   -SHI 3. -GA 4. -NA 3. : desid. comb. of suf-
            fix and parts. (follows renyōkei, -TE 1., or
            -NI 4.)

ika de kono Kaguyahime wo eteshigana (Tak.) : [they
all] wanted to win this Kaguyahime by hook or by crook

mienishigana to tsune ni koso oboyure (Mak.) : they
will certainly always want one to see that...

ika de mikikazu ni arinishigana to omou ni (Mak.) :
as I was wishing that somehow he might not hear about
it

samashihaberinishigana (GM) : I wanted to save [her]

SHIKA

1. **izenkei** of -KI 3. (follows **renyōkei** or sometimes
mizenkei)

    sate wa imijiku koso to oboeshika (Tsure.) : this
being the case, I was certainly delighted

    Betō owaseshikaba (Mak.) : since he was the Director

2. adv. : **thus, so**

    kokoro **shika** ni wa araji ka (Man.) : can it be that
those are not her feelings?

    shikajika no hito (Mak.) : such and such people

3. -SHI 3. -KA 4. (follows **renyōkei**)

    tsukasa kōburi kokoromoto naku oboeshi ka (Eiga) :
should I have doubts about rank and nobility? (lit.
did I probably have doubts...)

4. see ITSU SHIKA

5. -SHIKU 2. -A 4.

    ashikameri (Mak.) : this seems bad

-SHIKABA   -SHIKA 1. -BA 1.

    ōserareshikaba (Mak.) : because Her Majesty had said

    ame no imijū furishikaba (Mak.) : when it was raining
heavily

    Yodo no Watari to iu wo mono seshikaba (Mak.) : be-
cause we crossed on the Yodo Ferry

    toishikaba (Mak.) : when I asked

-SHIKADO(MO)   -SHIKA 1. -DO(MO)

    ōku kikoeshikado (Mak.) : though I have heard many
things

    jōko ni wa kayō ni arishikadomo (Hei.) : though this
is the way things were in the old days

-SHIKANARI   -SHIKU 2.   -ANARI

hito no kokorozashi hitoshikanari (Tak.) : people's
hopes are said to be all alike

SHIKAREDO(MO)   SHIKA 2.   -ARE 3.   DO(MO) : nevertheless,
yet, but

shikaredomo are wa wasureji (Hei.) : but I shall not
forget it

-SHIKI

1. rentaikei of shikukatsuyō adj.

   sawagashiki mono (Mak.) : noisy things

2. adj. suff. forming adjs. out of nouns, vbs., Chinese
   roots, etc.

   katakunashiki nyūdō no kokorobae (GM) : the disposition
   of a stubborn lay priest

-SHIKU

1. -SHI 3. -KU 2a.

   neshiku (Man.) : the fact that we slept

2. mizenkei and renyōkei of shikukatsuyō adj.

   anazurawashiku omoiyararete (Mak.) : regarding it
   scornfully

-SHIKUTE   -SHIKU 2.   -TE 1.

nakanaka uruwashikute (GM) : being very beautiful

-SHIME

izenkei and renyōkei of -SHIMU

yamabito no ware ni eshimeshi yamatsuto (Man.) : the
mountain ivy that the hermit (graciously) gave me

-SHIMI

stem of shikukatsuyō adj. -MI 2.

no wo natsukashimi (Man.) : because I found the wild moors so captivating

SHI MO   SHI 4.   -MO 3. : emph. comb. of parts.

nado ka wa sa shi mo uchitoketsuru (Mak.) : how can you be so terribly negligent?

saru hito shi mo (Mak.) : precisely people like that

...kokochi suru hodo ni shi mo (Mak.) : just as I was [beginning to] feel that...

-SHIMU

shūshikei of -shimu, causative and hon. shimonidan vb. suff. (follows mizenkei)

chōtei Yoshisada wo meshite Kyōto ni kaerashimu (Tai.) : the Court summoned Yoshisada back to Kyoto

-SHIMURU

rentaikei of -SHIMU

kokoro wo itamashimuru wa (Tsure.) : things that wound the heart

SHITARI   SHI 2.   -TARI 1.

shitarishigao (MSN) : a self-satisfied (lit. I've-gone-and-done-it) look

SHITE   SHI 2.   -TE 1.

1. case part.

(a) by, with, by means of, through

hibashi shite hasamu koto nashi (Tsure.) : they do not pick them up with tongs

105

SHITE 1a. (continued)

Yakugai to iu mono shite nomite (Mak.) : drinking
from a thing called a Yaku shell

ito nibuki katana shite kiru (Mak.) : to cut with an
extremely blunt blade

(b) indicating agent who is caused to do the action

Kogimi shite...kikoesasetari (GM) : he made Kogimi
tell them

Sakyō no Kimi shite shinobite tamawasetaritsuru (Mak.) :
she has sent it secretly through Lady Sakyō

(c) indicating an accompanying group

mutsumajiki kagiri shite owashimashinu (GM) : he proceeded [to that place] with all his intimate friends

2. conj. part. expressing condition, reason, etc. (follows renyōkei of adj.)

wakaku shite katachi no oitaru ni masareru (Tsure.) :
when one is young, one looks better than when one is
old

3. present participle

ōkata higashi wo makura to shite (Tsure.) : in general
the east is regarded as the pillow

mukotori shite shigonen made ubuya no sawagi senu
(Mak.) : having taken a husband for one's young daughter, one finds that several years later she still has
no child

sashinuki usuraka ni koromogae shite (GM) : changing
into a thin divided skirt

SHITSU   SHI 2.   -TSU 1.

madoi shitsuru (Mak.) : we have been embarrassed

SHI ZO   SHI 4.   ZO 1. : emph. comb. of parts.

tabi wo shi zo omou (Ise) : thinking of this (very)
journey

106

-SHŪ

ombin form of -SHIKU 2.

monosawagashū oboshimeshite (Eiga) : being agitated in
mind

ito tsukizukishū okashūte owasu (Mak.) : he was most
appropriately and pleasantly accoutred

SO

1. demonst. and pers. pron. : that, it; he, she

so ga iikeraku (Tosa) : what he said

2. expletive or emph. part. (vid. NA...SO, TA SO)

ko wa ta so to ieba (Mak.) : since he asked who it
could (possibly) be

SOKO

1. loc. adv. : there, in that direction

Nyōgo no Miya no soko ni owasureba (GM) : since
Princess Nyōgo was there

2. pers. pron., 2nd pers. : you

nao soko ni (Mak.) : [this is] after all for you

sokodomo sukoshi sare (Mak.) : you (people) there,
move back a little

-SOMU

aux. shimonidan vb. meaning to begin (follows renyōkei)

hototogisu ima kinakisomu (Man.) : now the hototogisu
is here and has begun to sing

SONATA

same as SOKO

sonata ni mukaite (Mak.) : turning in that direction

SO NE   see NA...SO (NE)

SONO   SO 1. -NO 1. : demonst. adj. : that, those; his

sono toshi sono tsuki (Mak.) : in that month and year

SORE

same as SO 1.

sore wo dani kimi ga katami to mitsutsu (Man.) : regarding it as a memento of you

sore watarasetamaite nochi (Mak.) : after Her Highness
had passed

SŌRŌ   see SABURAU

SU

shūshikei of su

1. sahen vb. meaning to do, make, be, wear, say, love,
prepare, bring, treat, handle, regard, etc.

nani su to mo naku (Mak.) : without appearing to do
anything

Hotoke no migi no kata ni chikaki ma ni shitari (GM) :
her room was to the right of the Buddha's statue

ashū serarete (Mak.) : being badly treated

hire kutai nado shite (Mak.) : they wear such things
as shoulder sashes and waistband ribbons

onaji koto shitaru (Mak.) : he says the same thing

imijū suru hito (Mak.) : a woman whom one loves dearly

ima hitotsu shite (Mak.) : now getting ready [another
carriage]

kakeban nado shite (Mak.) : they brought out small
tables

2. **shimonidan** suff. with same meaning as -SASU (follows **mizenkei** of **yodan**, **nahen**, and **rahen** vbs.)

    me no ōna ni azukete yashinawasu (Tak.) : he gave her to his wife to bring up

    to notamawasu (Mak.) : His Excellency said that...

3. aux. **sahen** vb. forming vb. out of subst., part., etc. (follows subst., part., etc.)

    maisu (Kok.) : to dance

    koesu (Man.) : to cry

SUGARA

suff. meaning **while, throughout**

    yo wa sugara ni shika zo nakunaru (Sōan Shū) : the deer cried all night long

    michisugara (Tsure.) : every step of the way

SUNAWACHI

adv. meaning **thereupon, accordingly; at once, immediately**

    umaretamaishi sunawachi yori (Uts.) : as soon as it was born

    yorokobi ni sunawachi mo mairamahoshiku haberishi wo (GM) : since I was pleased and immediately wanted to go

SURA

adv. part. : **as much as, at least, even**

    koto towanu ki sura (Man.) : even the trees, which lack the gift of speech

SURE

1. **izenkei** of SU

    kono yo no ajiki naki koto wo mōshishirasureba (GM) : when he informed him of the vanity of this world

SURE 1. (continued)

to notamawasuredomo (Mak.) : although Her Majesty said that...

2. izenkei of shimonidan vb. ending in -su

shinobite hikiyosuredo (Mak.) : though he steals up to her

SURU

1. rentaikei of SU

migurushi tote hito ni kakasuru wa urusashi (Tsure.) : it is a nuisance when they get other people to write for them because their own writing is bad

kuwasuru hito mo ito nikushi (Mak.) : people who invite (lit. cause) them to eat are also most hateful

2. rentaikei of shimonidan vb. ending in -su

uchiyosuru nami to tomo ni (Kok.) : together with the approaching waves

TA

1. interr. pron. : who?

ta ga tsuma (Koj.) : whose wife?

2. stem of -TASHI

...ni mo shitashi (Hei.) : I should like to regard it as...

3. intensifying pref.

shimo no ue ni arare tabashiri (Man.) : hail was pelting down on the frost

4. abbrev. of -TARI 1., -TARU

kao nado fukuretameri (Mak.) : his face seemed swollen

nekodono no mairita to wa nanigoto zo (Hei.) : what do you mean by saying that the cat has come?

110

TABU

1. shūshikei and rentaikei of yodan vb. tabu, and shūshi-kei of shimonidan vb. tabu, both meaning to eat, drink

mono mo etabade (Uts.) : being unable to eat anything

matsu no ha wo tabete (Sagoromo) : eating pine needles

2. shūshikei and rentaikei of yodan vb. tabu, having same meaning as TAMAU I.

waga se tsutometabubeshi (Man.) : my lover must be exerting himself

tabe sono zuzu shibashi (Mak.) : give us your rosary for a moment

Hyōe no Kurōdo ni tabitarikereba (Mak.) : when His Majesty gave it to the Lady Chamberlain Hyōe

TACHI

1. plur. suff. (mainly hon.)

onnatachi no go-uchi ni (GM) : among the ladies-in-waiting

2. vb. pref., often having a slight intensifying force but **

tachiyasuraubeki ni hata haberaneba (GM) : since I must not hesitate, however...

-TAGARU   -TA 2.   -GARU : desid. yodan vb. suff. (follows renyōkei)

o-mimairi ni iritagari (Uji) : wishing to go in and see

-TAKI

rentaikei of -TASHI

uchi ni aritaki ki (Tsure.) : trees I should like to have at home

Hidari no Ōidono no sabakari no medetaki on-ikioi nite (GM) : the Minister of the Left, having such impressive power...

111

-TAKU

mizenkei and renyōkei of -TASHI

Butsudō no shūgyō shitaku saburaedomo (GM) : though I
wish to practise Buddhism

TAMAE

1. izenkei and meireikei of TAMAU 1.

kaerigoto shitamae (GM) : pray write an answer

miyako ni sumasuru koto wo yurusasetamae (Mak.) :
grant that they be allowed to live in the capital

2. mizenkei and renyōkei of TAMAU 2.

mitamaeshikaba (GM) : if I had seen

mono no anata omoutamaeyarazarikeru ga (GM) : though I
did not think of [my mother's condition] in the next
world

TAMAERI

renyōkei and shūshikei of -ERI form of TAMAU 1.

komaka ni shitsuraimigakasetamaeri (GM) : he made [his
attendants] polish them carefully and install them

henji shite okasetamaerikeri (Mak.) : he wrote an
answer and ordered that it be delivered

TAMAERU

rentaikei of TAMAERI

hito kakushiokitamaeru naru beshi (GM) : they say that
His Excellency is keeping her in hiding

TAMAI

renyōkei of TAMAU 1.

nikushimi shitamaikeri (GM) : the Prince resented [her
behaviour]

112

TAMAU

1. shūshikei and rentaikei of tamau, yodan vb.

   (a) to give (to an inferior), bestow

   toridori ni tamau (GM) : His Excellency gave each of
   them

   (b) hon. aux. vb. (follows renyōkei)

   miya mo ito rōtaku shitamau (GM) : the Prince (also)
   was very fond of her

   In no mi-sajiki ni mairitamaite (Mak.) : [His Excel-
   lency] went to the gallery of the Empress Dowager and
   ...

2. shūshikei of tamau, shimonidan vb.

   (a) to drink, eat, receive*

   (b) humble or polite aux. vb. (mainly used after vbs.
   of thinking, seeing, hearing, etc., and in the Heian
   period mainly used humbly, i.e. of oneself; not
   normally found in shūshikei) (follows renyōkei)

   sutegataku omoitamaetsuru koto wa (GM) : the fact that
   I found it hard to forsake her

   aruji no musumedomo ōkari to kikitamaete (GM) : when I
   heard that the master had many daughters

   (see TAMAURU for further example)

TAMAURU

rentaikei of TAMAU 2.

   ...to namu kikitamauru (GM) : I have heard, Your
   Excellency, that...

TAMAUTE

same as TAMAI -TE

   aware ni mitatematsuritamaute (GM) : [Genji] felt sorry
   for [her] and...

TAMAWA

mizenkei of TAMAU 1.

nado ōgi woba tsukaitamawazatsuru zo to toikeru ni
(Hei.) : when he asked why he had not used his fan

TAMAWARU   TAMAWA -RU 2. (but. conjugated as yodan) : to
             give, bestow

tamawarasetamaikereba (GM) : since His Majesty was
graciously pleased to bestow

roku ōku tamawarishi koto (Mak.) : they rewarded me
with many presents

TAMAWASU   TAMAWA -SU 3. : to give, bestow

tamawasetaru mono wa onoono waketsutsu (Tak.) :
severally dividing the things that had been bestowed
on him

mono wo nagetamawasetaru (Mak.) : [Her Majesty] threw
something at me

-TAMERI   -TA 4. -MERI

to koso hito wa omoitamere (Mak.) : people must certainly have thought that...

fumi ni mo tsukuritameru (Mak.) : I believe that it has
also been described in a Chinese poem

TA MO   TA 1. MO 1. : everyone, all

ta mo...to nomi koso haberumere (Mak.) : indeed they
all seemed to be convinced that...

TAMŌ   see TAMAU

-TARA

mizenkei of -TARI
omi motte omi tarazumba arubekarazu (Hei.) : the retainer must behave as (lit. be) a retainer

114

-TARABA   -TARA   -BA la.

soshiraretaraba (Mak.) : if I were to be criticized

michi ni hito no aitaraba (Mak.) : if someone met us
on the way

-TARAMU   -TARA   -MU

tobi no itaramu nani ka wa kurushikarubeki (Tsure.) :
what does it matter that (or even if) the kites
remain?

asu kaeritaramu (Mak.) : [when] they have returned
tomorrow

ayashū naritaramu (Mak.) : it must have [seemed]
strange

-TARAZU   -TARA   -ZU 1.

isasaka hazukashi to mo omoitarazu (Mak.) : I did
not find it at all embarrassing

kimi kimi tarazu to iedomo (Hei.) : even if his lord
does not [behave like] a lord

TARE

1. izenkei and meireikei of -TARI

ōtonabura sashiidetareba (Mak.) : when they brought
out the great lamp

...koso imijiku mono wa shiritare (Mak.) : they
really know things extremely well

2. same as TA 1.

ima wa mata tare ka wa tote (GM) : who apart from me
will think about it now?

waga yo tare zo tsune naramu (iroha) : who indeed
will last forever in this world of ours?

-TAREBA   -TARE 1.   -BA 1b.

koshi agewatashitareba (Mak.) : because the lattices
have been opened

kyo wa Miya ni mairitareba (Mak.) : when I went to see
Her Majesty today

-TAREDO(MO)   -TARE 1.   -DO(MO)

Hitomaro nakunaritaredo (Kok.) : though Hitomaro has
died

hi wa idetaredo (Mak.) : though the sun had risen

-TARI

1. renyokei and shushikei of -tari (-TE 1. -ARI 1.), affirmative, emph., progressive, present, past, or perfective rahen vb. suff. (follows renyokei)

haraishitsurawaretari (GM) : they had been cleared
away

tai no hodo ni...sumaitari (Mak.) : he lives in a
wing of the house

2. renyokei and shushikei of -tari (TO 4. -ARI 1.), rahen
copula or affirmative vb. suff. (equiv. to modern de aru)
: is, are (follows subst. and uninfl. adj.)

mukashi koso sanzennin kanju tarishikadomo (Hei.) : in
the old days he was the leader of three thousand men,
but...

omi tarazumba (Hei.) : if he is not a retainer

-TARIKERI   -TARI 1.   -KERI

akatsuki ni kaozukurishitarikeru wo (MSN) : she had
made herself up at dawn

-TARIKI   -TARI 1.   -KI 3.

nochi yasuki mono ni oboshitariki ka shi (Hei.) :
later he really became convinced that it was an easy
thing

116

-TARISHI   -TARI 1. -SHI 3.

    Yoritomo wa moto wa futoritarishi ga (Hei.) : though
Yoritomo used to be sturdy

    yoku mo nitarishi ka na (Mak.) : she really does look
[like him], doesn't she?

-TARITSU   -TARI 1. -TSU 1.

    muge ni omoiwasuretaritsuru koto (Mak.) : a thing
that I had completely forgotten

-TARU

rentaikei of -TARI

    murasakidachitaru kumo no hosoku tanabikitaru
(Mak.) : wisps of purplish cloud trail [over
them]

    gaga taru gennan (Hei.) : precipitously steep
mountains

-TASHI

1. shūshikei of -tashi, desid. aux. kukatsuyō adj. (follows renyōkei)

    Sasaki-dono no nusumi wa aemono ni mo shitashi
(Hei.) : I should like to regard Lord Sasaki's thievery
as being of a similar nature

2. intensifying suff. (abbr. of itashi = "very") (follows
renyōkei)**

    ito medetashi (Mak.) : it is most admirable

TA SO   TA 1. -SO 2. : who indeed?

    ko wa ta so to ieba (Mak.) : since he asked who it
could (possibly) be

TATEMATSURU

shūshikei and rentaikei of yodan vb. tatematsuru

1. to make offerings, present; go, ride; write; put on clothing, wear; etc.

nishikawa yori tatematsureru ayu (GM) : trout that had been offered [to the Palace] from the western river

sore yori zo on-muma ni wa tatematsurikeru (GM) : from there he went on horseback

uchi mo mata haritaru mo amata tatematsurite (Mak.) : she was wearing several layers both of fulled and of stretched [silk]

on-ōgi tatematsurasetamau ni (Mak.) : when His Excellency presented his fan [to the Empress]

kaerigoto tatematsuramu tote (Mak.) : intending to write our reply

2. humble aux. vb. (follows renyōkei)

myōbu wa...aware ni mitatematsuru (GM) : the lady felt sorry [for the Emperor]

ware mo ichinichi mo mitatematsuranu wa (GM) : if I do not see you for a single day

sa namu to kikasetatematsuredo (Mak.) : though she informed her mistress accordingly

katarikikasetatematsure to nameri ka shi (Mak.) : they certainly seemed to be suggesting that I should tell you

TATOI

concessive conj. : even if, notwithstanding, though

kakaru rōboshi no mi ni wa tatoi ureehaberitomo nani no kui ka haberamu (GM) : how can an old priest like me have regrets even if I am sad [sometimes]?

-TATSU

aux. vb. meaning to begin (follows renyōkei)

mina sōzoku shitachite (Mak.) : beginning to put on
their costumes, they all...

maitachitaru (Mak.) : they began dancing

-TE

1. mizenkei and renyōkei of -TSU 1., having conj., parti-
cipial, perfective, adverbial, and certain specialized
uses (follows renyōkei)

tsutomete fune ni kuruma kakisuete watashite anata no
kishi ni kuruma hikitatete (Sara.) : on the following
morning they loaded the carriage on the boat, and,
having crossed over, placed it on the opposite bank

2. izenkei and meireikei of yodan vbs. ending in -tsu

aki wa higurashi no koe mimi ni miteri (Hoj.) : in the
autumn the singing of the cicadas fills my ears

3. mizenkei and renyōkei of shimonidan vbs. ending in -tsu

dojikidomo tatewatasu (MSN) : they distributed rice
balls and other dishes

-TEBA   -TE 1.   -BA la.

ume ga ka wo sode ni utsushite todometeba (Kok.) : if
one could transfer the scent of the plum blossoms to
one's sleeves and keep it there

TE FU   see CHŌ

-TEKERI   -TE 1.   -KERI

mina oikaeshitekeri (Tsure.) : they beat off all
[the enemy]

ge ni ayamachitekeri (Mak.) : I was indeed mistaken

-TEKI   -TE 1. -KI 3.

    hayō migushi oroshitamaiteki (Yam.) : he took holy
orders early

    hajime no wa...toritamaiteki (Mak.) : he took the first
of them

-TEMASHI   -TE 1. -MASHI

    ari no mama ni ya kikoetemashi (GM) : should she let
him know the whole situation?

    kokoro wo soe mo shitemashi (Mak.) : my heart would
have accompanied you

-TEMO   -TE 1. -MO 2.

    irihatetemo (GM) : even though you enter

    otona ni naritemo (Mak.) : even though he has grown up

-TEMU   -TE 1. -MU

    kono mi-kōshi wa sashitemu (GM) : let us shut (up)
this lattice door

    oni nado mo wa woba miyurushitemu (GM) : will the
devils let me go unscathed?

    tamawase mo shitemu (Mak.) : she will send [a carriage]
for us

-TE(MU) NOCHI   -TE 1. (MU) -nochi (conj. meaning "after")

    hikiinetemu nochi wa (Koj.) : after having (probably)
led her to bed

    sore watarasetamaite nochi (Mak.) : after Her Highness
had passed

-TEMU YA   -TEMU YA 1.

    sa wa imijū norou tomo uchihazushitemu ya (Mak.) : how
could anyone lose after reciting all those charms?

-TENU   -TE 1. -NU 1.

    kaku nagara chirade yo wo ya wa sugushitenu (Goshui) :
do you mean to say that [the blossoms] still did not
fall but passed through the night intact?

-TESHI   -TE 1. SHI 3.

    miteshi hito (Kok.) : she whom I saw

    denjōbito mina miteshi wa (Mak.) : all the senior
courtiers saw it

-TESHIGANA   see -SHIGANA

-TE YO   -TE 1. YO 2.

    kono yo wo sugushite yo to ya (Goshui) : are you
telling me to go through this life...?

TO

1. concessive conj. part. (follows shūshikei of vb. or
renyōkei of adj.) : even, even though, although

    aigyō naku to (Mak.) : even though they are not
attractive

    ho ni idetari to (Kage.) : although they came out in
rice-ears

    tomi no koto nari to (Mak.) : even though it is an
urgent matter

2. coordinating case part. : and, together with, along
with, with

    fuku kaze to tani no mizu to (Kok.) : the gusts of
wind and the water in the valleys

    kimi to oramashi mono wo (Man.) : oh, that I might be
with you!

    Kōgu Yama to Miminashi Yama to aishi toki (Mak.) :
when Mounts Kōgu and Miminashi come together

TO (continued)

3. particle

(a) marking end of subordinate clause (speech, narration; expression of thought, feeling, intention, etc.) (N.B. the vb. modified by the to clause is often omitted, as in three of the following examples)

wasuregusa shirushi ari ya to tsumite (Tosa) : picking a spray of "forgetfulness flower," I wondered whether it was really true to its name

omowazu ni kokoroushi to hazukashime (GM) : he put her to shame, saying, "What a terrible way to behave!"

kikoetemashi to obosedo (GM) : though she wondered whether she should tell him

yoki tokoro ni tatemu to isogaseba (Mak.) : wanting to find a good place [for my carriage], I made [my servants] hurry, and so...

kimi yuku to kikaba (Mak.) : if I had heard that you were going

(b) forming adv. phrases from onomatopoeias, duplicated, assonant, and other subst. forms

kita ni wa aoyama gaga to shite matsu fuku kaze sakusaku tari (Hei.) : in the north the green hills rose steeply and the wind soughed through the pine trees

tsurezure to ito mono kanashikute omowashikereba (Ise) : because you were languishing in gloomy idleness

yurari to koyuru (Tsure.) : to cross smoothly

soyosoyo to amata orite (Mak.) : several [women] came down with a rustling [of their silk clothes]

(c) expressing parity, similarity, condition, etc. : as, like, than

momiji wa ame to furutomo (Kok.) : though the maple leaves rain down (lit. fall like rain)

katachi nado wa kano mukashi no Yūgao to otoraji (GM) : she was no less beautiful than Yūgao had been (in the past)

sarusawa no ike no tamamo to miru zo kanashiki (Gosen):
it is sad indeed to see [her hair floating] like seaweed on Sarusawa Pond

nari to tsukureru aki no ta (Man.) : the autumn fields
which she is laying out as her task

yaku to...homekikoyuru ni (Mak.) : I praise you as if
that were my function [in life]

tazuki to mo seyo (Tsure.) : let us make it our livelihood

kimi ni niru kusa to mishi yori (Man.) : because the
plant reminded me of you

(d) indicating condition into which someone or something is changed

uzura to narite (Ise) : becoming (or being turned into) a quail

hana to mimashi ya (Kok.) : will probably come to see
them as blossoms

4. intensifying part. (follows renyōkei)

yo ni ari to aru hito wa (Mak.) : every single person
in the world

ki to kite wa (Tosa) : going ahead rapidly

5. conj. part. expressing time : when (follows rentaikei)
(abbrev. of toki = "time"?)

uma ineshi to (Nihon.) : when the horse slept

TŌBU

1. same as TAMAU 1.

sore wa Ryūen ni tōbe (Mak.) : give it to Ryūen

funaei shitōberishi mi-kao : His Highness' face which
[was green] from sea-sickness

2. same as TAMAU 2b.

kaku mōshitōbeba (Uts.) : when I said that

123

TŌBU 2. (continued)

hanahada hizō ni wa haberitōbu (GM) : it is highly
irregular

TO IU TO 3a. iu (yodan vb. : "to say," "to be called") :
phrase meaning to say that, have the name of; often
used to connect a modifier with a subst. form, in
which case **

mochizuki to iu mono (Mak.) : rice-cakes known as
mochizuki

genza to iu kagiri wa (MSN) : all the exorcists that
were [available]

TO KA TO 3a. KA 4. (N.B. kiku ("to hear"), omou ("to
think"), etc. are often understood)

akete matsu to ka (Mak.) : I have heard that [the
barrier] is open and awaits [the traveller]

medetaki mi ni naramu to ka (Mak.) : do you suppose
you will become a splendid person?

TOMO

1. same as TO 1. (follows shūshikei of vb. or renyōkei of
adj.)

chirinu tomo (Kok.) : though you end by scattering

adagataki nari tomo (GM) : though he is an enemy

imijū norō tomo (Mak.) : though it is extremely slow

tsuraki koto ari tomo (Mak.) : though things have been
painful

2. TO 3. -MO 1.

sekkyō nado shite yo wataru tazuki to mo seyo (Tsure.)
: let us make our livelihood by preaching

take no na to mo shiranu (Mak.) : I did not (even)
know that this was the name of bamboo

TO NAMU   TO 3a. NAMU 1. : comb. of parts. used in re-
          porting some astonishing or noteworthy statement,
          or to mark the end of a section, book, etc. (N.B.
          omou ("to think"), iu ("to say"), etc. are often
          understood)**

azumayama ni hijiri goranji ni to namu (GM) : a holy
man saw it in the eastern hills

TO NARI   TO 3d. NARI 3.

hitoyo ga hodo ni chirihai to nariniki (Hoj.) : became
dust and ashes in a matter of a single night

TO SHITE   TO 3c. SHITE 2. : as

ōyakebito to shite haberishi (Uts.) : I was acting as
(or in the capacity of) a courtier

TO SU   TO 3c. SU 1. : phrase expressing intention or ef-
         fort (usually follows -MU)

tsuraku miyuredo kokorozashi semu to su (Tosa) : though
it appeared hard to bear, I tried to take it well

mono iwamu to suru ni mo (Mak.) : though one is on the
verge of saying something

TOTE

1. contr. of TO 3a. - [omoi ("thinking"), etc.] -TE 1. :
seeing (thinking, saying, hearing, etc.) that, regarding
[something] as

nakibito no kuru yoru tote (Tsure.) : as the night on
which the dead return

morotomo ni tote on-kayukowa iimeshite (GM) : he decided that they would [dine] together and he ordered
rice to be served

...tote ine to iu mono ōku toriidete (Mak.) : so saying, he sent for several rice plants

hajime wa on-tsuwari tote mono mo kikoshimesazarikeru
ni (Eiga) : thinking at first that it was a [mere] in-
disposition Her Majesty did not mention it, but...

TOTE 1. (continued)

onna mo shite mimu tote suru nari (Tosa) : a woman too
will try her hand at it

akatsuki ni iku tote (Mak.) : hearing that she was
going to leave at dawn

go wo...utsu tote (Mak.) : about (or intending) to
play a game of go

2. conj. : although (contr. of TO 3a. -ii ("saying")
-TE[MO])

ware nakinarinu tote (GM) : though I die

monooshimi sesasetamau miya tote (Mak.) : though Your
Majesty is a stingy Empress

TO WA   TO 3a. WA 1.

makoto ni oboshikeri to wa kore nite koso shirinure
(Mak.) : from this I certainly know that you (really)
hold me in high regard

TO YA

same as TO NAMU**

hashitanakameri to ya (GM) : it must have been unseemly

medekeri to ya (GM) : they praised it

TO ZO

same as TO NAMU**

to zo hon ni haberumeru (GM) : thus it is written in
the book

to ōserareshikaba to zo (Mak.) : it was indeed because
Her Majesty had said that...

TSU

1. shūshikei of -tsu, affirmative, emph., past, or progressive shimonidan vb. suff. (generally affixed to
transitive vbs.) (follows renyōkei)

waga koi wa nagusamekane_tsu_ (Man.) : my love cannot
be appeased

on-fumi wa torasetamai_tsu_ (Mak.) : Her Majesty took the
letter

ire_tsu_ (Mak.) : I let him in

nami mo koe tate_tsu_ (Hei.) : even the waves have
raised their voices

mi_tsu_ ya (Mak.) : did you see?

2. genitive case part., also used as a numerical classi-
fier

hiru_tsu_kata (Mak.) : at about noon

oki _tsu_ nami (Man.) : the waves far out at sea

itsu_tsu_ ginu kitaru nyōbo (Hei.) : a lady-in-waiting
wearing five layers of robes

-TSUBESHI   -TSU 1.   -BESHI

nami tate_tsubeshi_ (Tosa) : they (certainly) made the
waves stand up

hashiri mo uchi_tsubeshi_ (Mak.) : I should certainly
run after him and hit him

amari migurushi to mo mi_tsubeku_ wa aranu (Mak.) :
they cannot have been too unpleasant to see

TSUKAEMATSURU

humble _yodan_ vb. : to serve, _do_, perform

Ōigimi ni kataku tsukaematsururamu (GM) : (probably)
serves Her Ladyship diligently

sayō no koto ni _tsukaematsuru_ hito mo naki ni ya
(Hei.) : you mean to say that you do not have people
to perform jobs like that?

TSUKETE   see NI TSUKETE

TSUKŌMATSURU

same as TSUKAEMATSURU

ware koso kono kawari mo tsukōmatsurame (Eiga) : I myself shall perform the office in her place

akekure omae ni saburaitsukōmatsuru koto mo oboezu
(Mak.) : I forget that I am (serving) in the Imperial
presence day and night

katame mo akitsukōmatsurade wa (Mak.) : [since] I am
entirely illiterate (lit. neither of my eyes is open)

-TSURAMU   -TSU 1. -RAMU 1.

nadote kono tsukigoro mōdede sugushitsuramu to (Mak.) :
wondering why they had let all these months go by without visiting the temple

ika de kikitamaitsuramu to (Mak.) : wondering how he
could [possibly] have heard

hito ni ya misetsuramu (Mak.) : I wonder whether he
has shown it to anyone

-TSURE

izenkei of -TSU 1.

toshi wo hete kimi wo nomi koso nesumitsure (Shui) :
over the years I have consorted with not a single man
but you

miiretsureba (Mak.) : when I looked in

imijiku mono koso aware naritsure (Mak.) : things were
certainly most moving

-TSURU

rentaikei of -TSU 1.

amata mietsuru kodomo (GM) : most children that he had
seen

sono tokoro ni kurashitsuru yoshi nado iu (Mak.) : he
said something to the effect that he had spent the
whole day in that place

nagokaritsuru umi (Mak.) : the sea, which had been calm

-TSUTSU

conj. part. expressing simultaneous action, continuation; repetition (follows renyōkei)

omoitsutsu nereba (Kok.) : since I went to sleep thinking [of my beloved]

take wo toritsutsu yorozu no koto ni tsukaikeri (Tak.) : he collected bamboo and (or collecting bamboo, he) put it to various uses

me wo kubaritsutsu yomiitaru (Mak.) : while glancing [at the women], he read [the sutras]

sode no shita...hikiyaritsutsu (Mak.) : he pushes back the bottom of his sleeve again and again

U

1. shūshikei infl. (follows stem of vbs.)

aware ni mitatematsuru (GM) : she felt sorry [for him]

2. shūshikei of u

(a) shimonidan vb. meaning to acquire, put to use

shukke muryō .no kōtoku u to ieru (Hei.) : they say that by becoming a monk one acquires boundless merit

(b) aux. shimonidan vb. expressing ability, possibility (follows renyōkei)

shimashiku mo hitori ariuru mono (Man.) : a person who can be alone for some time

3. ombin form of -MU (N.B. sō = sa-u)

uchiwaraiowasōzu (GM) : His Excellency was about to burst into laughter

4. see -FU

129

UCHI-

vb. pref. often having slight intensifying force**

honoka ni uchihikarite yuku mo okashi (Mak.) : I like
it when [a few fireflies] fly about glimmering dimly

uchinakasetamau (Mak.) : His Excellency wept (copiously)

WA

1. selective, separative, or distinguishing part., marking
the emphasis in a word or phrase and sometimes conveying a
cond. sense

ayashiki ie no midokoro mo naki mume no ki nado ni wa
kashigamashiki made zo naku (Mak.) : [uguisu] sing - -
and sing loudly - - in the plum-tree of some poor, in-
significant house (i.e. rather than anywhere else)

onoko wa tsuma wa hitori ya mochitaru (Eiga) : a man
has one wife

ōmi-koto wa uketamau (Shoku) : I hearken to the August
Word

ichinichi mo mitatematsuranu wa (GM) : if I do not see
you for a single day

e mairazu wa (Mak.) : if we cannot go

koishiku wa (Kok.) : if you long to see me

kuru hito mo aru wa (Mak.) : if someone came [to the
house]

kitaramu wa (Mak.) : if he should come

2. at end of sentence : interj. or interr. part.

ikaga wa semu wa (Ise) : oh, what shall I do?

arikumeru wa (Mak.) : they certainly seem to go!

kano hana usenikeru wa (Mak.) : good heavens, those
flowers have disappeared!

3. pers. pron., 1st pers. : I

wa wo shinoburashi (Man.) : she seems to love me

130

WADONO

  pers. pron., 2nd pers. : you

  wadono no rōjū (Hei.) : a retainer of yours

WAGA   WA 3. -GA 1. : my

  waga Ōkimi (Man.) : my Lord

WAGOZE

  pers. pron., 2nd pers. : thou, you (of women)

  wagoze no idasaretamaishi wo mishi ni tsukete mo
  (Hei.) : even when I saw that you had been sent
  away

WA MO YA   WA 1. MO 3. YA 2. : emph. or interj. comb. of
            parts.*

  ware wa mo ya Yasumiko etari (Man.) : I was the one
  who got Yasumiko

WARE

  pers. pron., 1st pers. : I

  ware mo ichinichi mo mitatematsuranu wa (GM) :
  I too, if I do not see you for a single
  day...

WA YA   WA 2. YA 1. : interj. comb. of parts.

  omou wa ya (Mak.) : I do indeed love you

WE

interj. or impera. part.*

  ware wa sabushi we kimi ni shi araneba (Man.) : ah,
  how sad that it is not my lord!

WO

1. objective case part.

   uma wo hikiidasasekeru ni ashi wo soraete shikimi wo
   yurari to koyuru wo mite wa (Tsure.) : when he saw him
   leading out his horse and smoothly crossing the thres-
   hold with his legs together

   koto wo kikabaya to omou ni (Mak.) : though I wanted to
   hear [their verdict]

2. conj. part. with extended use as concessive or causal
conj. part. (follows rentaikei) : and, though; since

   shibashi wa yume ka to nomi tadoraseshi wo yoyo omoi-
   shizumaru (GM) : for a time he could only feel that he
   was moving about in a dream, but eventually he became
   calmer

   toiawasubeki hito dani naki wo (GM) : since he had no
   one to consult

3. interj. or emph. part.

   kono yo naru ma wa tanoshiku wo ara na (Man.) : while
   we are in this world, let us be happy!

   ajiki naki kotodomo wo (Mak.) : there is really nothing
   interesting about all that

   nadote iu ni ka aramu wo (Mak.) : why on earth should
   she say this?

WOBA   WO 1. -WA 1. : emph. obj. comb. of parts.

   onore woba shirazaru nari (Tsure.) : he does not know
   me

   kirakirashiki nado woba e sa shimo oshihishigazu ka
   shi (Mak.) : the elegant [carriages] of course could
   not be treated in such a cavalier fashion

WO SHI   WO 1. SHI 4. : same as WOBA

   fune wo shi zo omou (Kok.) : I long for the ship

132

1. interr. adv. part. denoting uncertainty, used in rhet. questions,_statements of doubt or surprise, etc. (usually follows shūshikei and precedes rentaikei)

waga omou hito wa ari ya nashi ya (Kok.) : is my loved one there or 'not?

niguru hito wa shibashi to ya iu (Tsure.) : does someone who is hurrying away say he will be back shortly?

goban haberi ya (Mak.) : is there a go board here?

Hamana no hashi mizariki ya (Mak.) : do you suppose I have never seen the bridge of Hamana?

2. vocative or interj. part. (often follows or precedes izenkei and used in poetry to denote condition, comparison, likeness, etc. as in nare ya)

momoshiki no ōmiyabito wa itoma are ya (Man.) : it is (forsooth) because they have so much leisure that the courtiers of the august Palace...

kami mo ureshi to shinobazarame ya (Shui) : even the gods will be o'erwhelmed with joy

kuchioshi no koto ya (Mak.) : this is indeed a shame

okashikaranu koto zo naki ya (Mak.) : it was really not without charm

3. coordinating case part.

ayashige naru yuzu ya nashi ya nado wo...motarite (Kage.) : carrying plain-looking fruit - - citrons, pears, and the like

-YAKA

subst. suff. (follows renyōkei or adj. stem)

kezayaka nite (Mak.) : being clear

ōkiyaka naru warawa (Mak.) : a heavily built girl

YA MO   YA 1.-2.   MO 3. : same as KA MO 1.-2.

nioi wa sutomo utsurowame ya mo (Man.) : the colour is
beautiful, but will it not, alas, fade?

ware koime ya mo (Shui) : [in that case] would I
languish for you [as I do]?

YA WA   YA 1. WA 2. : same as KA WA

shiranu hito ya wa aru (Mak.) : can there be anyone
who does not know?

sa ya wa aru (Mak.) : one hardly expects to find you
[in this state]

YO

1. interj. or voc. part.

Shōnagon yo (Mak.) : oh, Shōnagon!

hito no monoiisaganasa yo (GM) : oh, the spitefulness
of people!

2. impera. or permissive part. (follows renyōkei of vbs.
other than yodan, nahen, and rahen)

hito ni naosaseyo (Mak.) : tell them to repair it

toku oriyo (Mak.) : get out [of your carriages] quickly

hito ni miseyo (Mak.) : show it to someone

3. same as YU 1.

matsubara yo miwataseba (Man.) : when you survey it
from the pine grove

YOMO

adv. : on no account, hardly

sōzu wa yomo sayō ni wa suetamawaji (GM) : a priest
would hardly have arranged things like that

YORI

same as KARA 1.-2. with extended meaning of <u>more than</u>

mi wo yaburu <u>yori</u> kokoro wo itamashimuru wa hito wo
sokonau koto nao hanahadashi. Yamai wo ukuru koto mo
oku wa kokoro <u>yori</u> uku. Soto <u>yori</u> kuru yamai wa suku-
nashi (Tsure.) : It hurts a person far more when you
pain his heart than when you wound his body. Illness
most often comes from the heart; it is rare that it
comes from the outside

utadomo <u>yori</u> wa okashi (Mak.) : it was more charming
than the poems

YOSHIYA

conj. part. : <u>even if</u>, <u>although</u>

Yoshinokawa <u>yoshiya</u> hito koso tsurakarame (Kok.) : even
though Yoshino River itself is willing enough, it is
the people who (will) suffer

YO YA   YO 1. YA 2. : voc. or interj. comb. of parts.

are mise <u>yo ya</u> haha (Mak.) : let me see that, Mummy!

YU

1. same as KARA 1.*

hina no nagamichi <u>yu</u> koikureba (Man.) : when I
travelled down the long road from the provinces, full
of love for you...

2. same as -RU 2. (follows <u>mizenkei</u>)

kimi ga kokoro wa wasura<u>yu</u>mashiji (Man.) : I cannot
forget your feelings

omowamu hito no kinu ni sura<u>yu</u> na (Man.) : let it not
be rubbed on the clothes of anyone who does not love
me!

3. <u>shushikei</u> of certain vbs.

okashu mi<u>yu</u> (Mak.) : it looks delightful

YUME...NA

neg. impera. constr. : <u>do not on any account</u>, <u>do not</u>

  <u>yume</u> hana chiru <u>na</u> (Man.) : oh, that the blossoms may not fall!

YURI

same as YU 1.*

  asu <u>yuri</u> ya (Man.) : from tomorrow indeed

-ZA

abbr. of -ZARI or -ZARU

  yamugoto naki sama ni wa motenashitamawazanaredo (GM) : though he was evidently not treatīng her as if she were of great [social]importance

-ZAMERI   -ZA -MERI

  tagawazameri to oboyu (Mak.) : it seemed to me that it was (probably) not different

  hiru dani kizameri (Mak.) : they do not seem to wear them even in the daytime

-ZARA

<u>mizenkei</u> of -ZARI

  miezaranu (Man.) : it is not unseen (i.e. is visible)

-ZARAMU   -ZARA -MU

  ikaga omowazaramu to oboyu (Mak.) : one wonders how they could possibly not love them

  kami mo ureshi to shinobazarame ya (Shui) : even the gods will be o'erwhelmed with joy (<u>lit.</u> will probably not be able to bear)

-ZARANU   -ZARA   -NU : comb. of neg. suffs. (i.e. double
         negative)

   miezaranu (Man.) : is visible

-ZARE

izenkei of -ZARI

   hito ni majiwarazareba (Hoj.) : since I do not
   associate with others

-ZAREDO(MO)   -ZARE   -DO(MO)

   awazaredo (Man.) : though we do not meet

-ZARI

renyōkei and shūshikei of -zari, neg. rahen vb. suff.
(= ZU I. -ARI Ib.) (follows mizenkei)

   ekikazarikeri (Ise) : was unable to hear

-ZARIKERI   -ZARI   -KERI 1.

   moe wa tsukazarikeru (Mak.) : the flames have not
   broken out

   shirazarikeru yo (Mak.) : you really did not know
   it!

-ZARIKI   -ZARI   -KI 3.

   Hamana no hashi mizariki ya (Mak.) : do you
   suppose I have never seen the bridge of
   Hamana?

-ZARISHI   -ZARI   -SHI 3.

   mada mairazarishi toki (Mak.) : before I entered
   Court service (lit. the time when I was not yet
   coming [to the palace])

137

-ZARITSU   -ZARI   -TSU 1.

ne mo irazaritsuru wo (Mak.) : since they do not fall
asleep

kanashisa nagusamubeki mo arazaritsu (Goshui) :
nothing remained that could relieve the sadness

-ZARU

rentaikei of -ZARI

chisha no sezaru tokoro nari (Tsure.) : it is something that wise people do not do

-ZE

mizenkei of -ZU 2.

chi no nagaruru made chōzesasetamau (Tak.) : he
ordered him to be flogged until the blood flowed

Ue mo Miya mo kyōzesasetamau (Mak.) : both Their
Majesties were delighted

ZO

1. emph. adv. part. (usually precedes and follows
rentaikei)**

yume no uchi ni mo hana zo chirikeru (Kok.) : even in
my dreams the petals were scattering

tare zo tsune naramu (iroha) : who indeed will last
forever?

otokogimi hitori zo owasuru (Ōkagami) : the gentleman
was (indeed) present

2. expletive, interj., or interr. part. (at end of
sentence)

izuko yori kitarishi mono zo (Man.) : whence does this
(thing) come?

maro wa nanatabi mōdeshihaberu zo (Mak.) : I mean to
do the pilgrimage seven times

138

ZO KA SHI   ZO 2.   KA SHI : emph. comb. of parts.

tada katasoba zo ka shi (GM) : they really give only one side of the story

so zo ka shi to miyuru hito (Mak.) : a certain man whom I certainly felt I had seen [before]

higagoto mo idekuru zo ka shi (Mak.) : mistakes are certainly likely to occur

ZO YA

1. ZO 2. YA 2. : interj. comb. of parts.

kono kawa wa Saikoku ichi no taiga zo ya (Hei.) : forsooth, this is one of the biggest rivers in the West

ge ni mo to oboesaburaishi zo ya (Hei.) : "How true!" I thought (indeed)

2. ZO 2. YA 1.

ika ni zo ya (Mak.) : how can that possibly be?

-ZU

1. mizenkei, renyōkei, and shūshikei of -zu, irregular neg. vb. suff. (follows mizenkei)

yamazu (Man.) : ceaselessly

sakashiku mo arazu (Kok.) : it is not clever

2. same as -SU 3. (follows subst.)

machikōzuru (Mak.) : waiting fretfully

3. shūshikei of -zu, intensifying aux. sahen vb. (follows mizenkei or -MU or -U 3.**

uchiwaraiowasōzu (= sa-u-zu) (GM) : His Excellency was about to burst out laughing

kanarazu semuzuramu to (Mak.) : [thinking] that I am quite sure to do it

-ZU 3. (continued)

mata makarazu to iite tachinu (Tosa) : he left, saying
that he would come again

(see -MUZU for further examples)

-ZUBA   -ZU 1. -BA la.

shinji nado ni haberazuba (Mak.) : unless you are a
scholar

kasane narazuba (Mak.) : if he does not [have] a many-
tiered box

-ZUMBA

same as -ZUBA with euphonic intercalation

omi motte omi tarazumba arubekarazu (Hei.) : the retainer must behave as a retainer

-ZURU

1. rentaikei of -ZU 2.

machikōzuru (Mak.) : waiting fretfully

2. rentaikei of -ZU 3.

kakaramuzuru koto to wa omoishikado (GM) : though he
expected it would really happen like that

...ni zo komuzuru (Mak.) : I shall come when...

-ZUTE   -ZU 1. -TE 1. : same as -DE

me ni wa miezute (Kok.) : being unable to see

kimi kozute toshi wa kureniki (Goshui.) : the year
ended without your coming

Appendixes

Appendix I: Conjugation of Type Verbs and Adjectives

Verbs

a. regular

	mizenkei	renyōkei	shūshikei	rentaikei	izenkei	meireikei	"stem"
kamiichidan (miru = to see)	mi	mi	miru	miru	mire	miyo	mir
kaminidan (oku = to rise)	oki	oki	oku	okuru	okure	okiyo	ok
yodan (yuku = to go)	yuka	yuki	yuku	yuku	yuke	yuke	yuk
shimonidan (tabu = to eat)	tabe	tabe	tabu	taburu	tabure	tabeyo	tab
shimoichidan (keru = to kick)	ke	ke	keru	keru	kere	keyo	ker

b. irregular

	mizenkei	renyōkei	shūshikei	rentaikei	izenkei	meireikei	"stem"
nahen (shinu = to die)	shina	shini	shinu	shinuru	shinure	shine	shin
rahen (ori = to be)	ora	ori	ori	oru	ore	ore	or
kahen (ku = to come)	ko	ki	ku	kuru	kure	ko(yo)	k

	se	shi	su	suru	sure	seyo	s
sahen (su = to do)							
Adjectives							
kukatsuyō (yoshi = good)	yoku	yoku	yoshi	yoki	yokere		yo
shikukatsuyō (utsukushi = beautiful)	utsuku-shiku	utsuku-shiku	utsuku-shi	utsuku-shiku	utsuku-shikere		utsuku-shi

143

Appendix II: Conjugation of Forms Included in List

	mizenkei	renyōkei	shūshikei	rentaikei	izenkei	meireikei
-BAMU (yodan)	bama	bami	bamu	bamu	bame	—
-BESHI (kukatsuyō)	beku	beku	beshi	beki	bekere	—
-BU (kaminidan)	bi	bi	bu	buru	bure	biyo
-DATSU (yodan)	data	dachi	datsu	datsu	date	—
ERI (rahen)	era	eri	eri	eru	ere	ere
-GAMASHI (shikukatsuyō)	gamashiku	gamashiku	gamashi	gamashiki	gamashikere	—
-GARU (yodan)	gara	gari	garu	garu	gare	—
-GATASHI (kukatsuyō)	gataku	gataku	gatashi	gataki	gatakere	—
-GOTOSHI (kukatsuyō)	gotoku	gotoku	gotoshi	gotoki	gotokere	—
HABERI (rahen)	habera	haberi	haberi	haberu	habere	—

HATSU (shimonidan)	hate	hate	hatsu	hatsuru	hatsure	—
IMASU (yodan)	imasa	imashi	imasu	imasu	imase	imase
IMASU (shimonidan)	imase	imase	imasu	imasuru	imasure	imaseyo
IRU (kamiichidan)	i	i	iru	iru	ire	iyo
-KANU (shimonidan)	kane	kane	kanu	kanuru	kanure	—
-KERI (rahen)	kera	—	keri	keru	kere	—
-KI (irregular)	se (ke ?)	—	ki	shi	shika	—
-KIKOESASU (shimonidan)	kikoesase	kikoesase	kikoesasu	kikoesasuru	kikoesasure	kikoesaseyo
-KIKOYU (shimonidan)	kikoe	kikoe	kikoyu	kikoyuru	kikoyure	kikoeyo
-KOSU (yodan)	kosa	koshi	kosu	kosu	kose	kose
-KUDASARU (shimonidan)	kudasare	kudasare	kudasuru	kudasaruru	kudasarure	kudasareyo
-MAHOSHI (shikukatsuyō)	mahoshiku	mahoshiku	mahoshi	mahoshiki	mahoshikere	—

	mizenkei	renyōkei	shūshikei	rentaikei	izenkei	meireikei
-MAIRASU (shimonidan)	mairase	mairase	mairasu	mairasuru	mairasure	mairaseyo
-MAIRU (yodan)	maira	mairi	mairu	mairu	maire	maire
-MAJI (shikukatsuyō)	majiku	majiku	maji	majiki	majikere	-
-MASHI (irregular)	mase	-	mashi	mashi	mahika	-
-MASU (yodan)	masa	mashi	masu	masu	mase	mase
-MATSURU (yodan)	matsura	matsuri	matsuru	matsuru	matsure	-
-MEKASHI (shikukatsuyō)	mekashiku	mekashiku	mekashi	mekashiki	mekashikere	-
-MEKU (yodan)	meka	meki	meku	meku	meke	-
-MERI (rahen)	mera	meri	meri	meru	mere	-
-MESU (yodan)	mesa	meshi	mesu	mesu	mese	-

	mono se	mono shi	mono su	mono suru	mono sure	mono seyo
MONO SU (sahen)	mono se	mono shi	mono su	mono suru	mono sure	mono seyo
-MŌSU (yodan)	mōsa	mōshi	mōsu	mōsu	mōse	mōse
-MU (yodan)	ma	–	mu	mu	me	–
NARI (rahen)	nara	nari	nari	naru	nare	nare
NARU (yodan)	nara	nari	naru	naru	nare	nare
NARU (shimonidan)	nare	nare	naru	naruru	narure	nareyo
-NASARU (shimonidan)	nasare	nasare	nasaru	nasaruru	nasarure	nasareyo
-NASHI (kukatsuyō)	naku	naku	nashi	naki	nakere	–
-NASU (yodan)	nasa	nashi	nasu	nasu	nase	nase
NOTAMAU (yodan)	notamawa	notamai	notamau	notamau	notamae	notamae
-NU (nahen)	na	ni	nu	nuru	nure	ne

	mizenkei	renyōkei	shūshikei	rentaikei	izenkei	meireikei
OBOSHIMESU (yodan)	oboshimesa	oboshimeshi	oboshimesu	oboshimesu	oboshimese	oboshimese
OBOSU (yodan)	obosa	oboshi	obosu	obosu	obose	obose
-OWASU (shimonidan)	owase	owase	owasu	owasuru	owasure	owaseyo
-OWASU (yodan)	owasa	owashi	owasu	owasu	owase	owase
-RAMU (yodan)	—	—	ramu	ramu	rame	—
-RARU (shimonidan)	rare	rare	raru	raruru	rarure	rareyo
-RASHI (shikukatsuyō)	rashiku	rashiku	rashi	rashiki	rashikere	—
-RAYU (shimonidan)	rae	rae	rayu	rayuru	rayure	raeyo
-RU (shimonidan)	re	re	ru	ruru	rure	reyo
-SABURAU (yodan)	saburawa	saburai	saburau	saburau	saburae	saburae

148

SARI (rahen)	sara	sari	saru	saru	sare	sare
-SASU (shimonidan)	sase	sase	sasu	sasuru	sasure	saseyo
SASU (yodan)	sasa	sashi	sasu	sasu	sase	sase
-SHI (kukatsuyō)	ku	ku	shi	ki	kere	—
-SHI (shikukatsuyō)	shiku	shiku	shi	shiki	shikere	—
-SHIMU (shimonidan)	shime	shime	shimu	shimuru	shimure	shimeyo
-SOMU (shimonidan)	some	some	somu	somuru	somure	someyo
-SŌRŌ (yodan)	see -SABURAU					
SU (sahen)	se	shi	su	suru	sure	seyo
-SU (shimonidan)	se	se	su	suru	sure	seyo
-TABU (yodan)	taba	tabi	tabu	tabu	tabe	tabe

	mizenkei	renyōkei	shūshikei	rentaikei	izenkei	meireikei
TABU (shimonidan)	tabe	tabe	tabu	taburu	tabure	tabeyo
-TAGARU (yodan)	tagara	tagari	tagaru	tagaru	tagare	tagare
-TAMAERI (rahen)	tamaera	tamaeri	tamaeri	tamaeru	tamaere	—
-TAMAU (yodan)	tamawa	tamai	tamau	tamau	tamae	tamae
-TAMAU (shimonidan)	tamae	tamae	tamau	tamauru	tamaure	tamaeyo
TAMAWARU (yodan)	tamawara	tamawari	tamawaru	tamawaru	tamaware	tamaware
-TARI (rahen)	tara	tari	tari	taru	tare	tare.
-TASHI (kukatsuyō)	taku	taku	tashi	taki	takere	—
-TATEMATSURU (yodan)	tatematsura	tatematsuri	tatematsuru	tatematsuru	tatematsure	tatematsure
-TŌBU (yodan)	tōba	tōbi	tōbu	tōbu	tōbe	tōbe

150

	te	te	tsu	tsuru	tsure	teyo
-TSU (shimonidan)	te	te	tsu	tsuru	tsure	teyo
TSUKAEMATSURU (yodan)	tsukaema-tsura	tsukaema-tsuri	tsukaema-tsuru	tsukaema-tsuru	tsukaema-tsure	tsukaema-tsure
-U (shimonidan)	e	e	u	uru	ure	eyo
-YU (shimonidan)	e	e	yu	yuru	yure	eyo
-ZARI (rahen)	zara	zari	zari	zaru	zare	zare
-ZU (irregular)	zu	zu	zu	nu	ne	--
-ZU (sahen)	ze	ji	zu	zuru	zure	zeyo

Appendix III: Selection of Forms Included in List
(classified according to grammatical function)

Independent Words (jiritsugo)

a. pronouns (fukumeishi)

personal, 1st person : a, are, onore, wa, wadono, ware

personal, 2nd person : imashi, kimuji, mimashi, na,
namuchi, omoto, onore, wagoze

personal, 3rd person : ka, kare

demonstrative and locative : ko, kochi, koko, konata,
kore; so, sonata, sore; a, are, ka, kare; achi, anata,
ashiko, asoko, kanata, kashiko

interrogative : izuchi, izukata, izuko, nani, nanigashi, ta, tare

b. adverbs (fukushi)

ikade (ka), ito, nao, shika

c. interjections (kandōshi)

ana, aware, ide, ika ni, iza

d. copulas (keiyō dōshi)

nari, tari

Auxiliary Words (fuzokugo)

a. auxiliary verbs and adjectives (jodōshi)

i. causative (shieki) : sasu, shimu, su

ii. passive (ukemi) : raru, ru

iii. honorific : see App. IV

iv. humble : see App. IV

v. polite : see App. IV

vi. negative (uchikeshi) : zari, zu

152

vii. desiderative (gambō) : mahoshi, tashi

viii. perfective (kaisō) : keri, ki

ix. past, emphatic, or progressive (kanryō) : eri, nu, tari, tsu

x. probability (yoryō) : ji, mu

xi. conjecture (kasō) : mashi

xii. supposition (suiryō) : beshi, kemu, maji, meri, ramu, rashi

xiii. report (dembun) : nari

xiv. comparison (hikyō) : gotoshi

xv. continuation (keizoku) : fu

b. particles (joshi)

i. substantival (juntai) : ga, ku, no

ii. case (kaku) : e, ga, kara, ni, nite, no, shite, tote, tsu, wo, yo, yori, yu, yuri

iii. coordinating (heiritsu) : to, ya

iv. conjunctive (setsuzoku) : ba, de, do, domo, ga, mono kara, mono wo, mono yue, nagara, ni, shite, te, to, tomo, tsutsu, wo

v. adverbial (fuku) : bakari, dani, made, nado, nomi, sae, shi, shi mo, sura

vi. emphatic, etc. (kei) : ka, ka mo, ka wa, koso, mo, namu, wa, ya, zo*

vii. interjectional, etc. (shū) : baya, ga, ka, ka mo, ka na, ka shi, mo ga mo, mo ga na, na, namu, na...so, ne, nishiga na, shika, teshiga na, ya

viii. imperative, etc. (kantō) : mo, we, wo, yo

* The rule of kakari-musubi : ka, namu, ya, and zo are normally followed by rentaikei infls.; koso is followed by an izenkei infl.

153

<u>particles</u> (continued)

    ix. plural (fukusū) : bara, dachi, domo, tachi

     x. intensifying : hiki, i, kai, mote, sashi, ta, tachi, uchi

    xi. honorific : go, mi, o, ōmi, on

Honorific (sonkei)

asobasu, imasu, kudasaru, masu, mesu, nasaru, nasu, owasu, raru, ru, sasu, shimu, su, tamau (yodan), tamawaru, tōbu

Polite (teinei)

haberi, saburau, tamau (shimonidan)

Humble (kenson)

kikoesasu, kikoyu, mairasu, matsuru, mōsu, saburau, tamau (shimonidan), tatematsuru

N.B. Honorific: indicates respect for doer of action (cf. modern o- ni naru)

Polite: indicates formal attitude to interlocutor, regardless of doer of action (cf. modern -masu, gozaimasu)

Humble: indicates lack of respect for doer of action, and respect for person to or for whom the action is done (cf. modern mōshiageru)